# MESSAGING

From my Pastor to me and
from your Pastor to you.
**12/25/17**

*Pastor David V. Hohlbaugh*

# MESSAGING

## WHY AUDIENCE MATTERS

JOHN WOOTTON

## Messaging

Address all inquiries to:
John Wootton
8405 Pulsar Pl, Suite 200
Columbus, OH 43240
info@messagingbook.com
www.messagingbook.com

Edited by Dean Merrill
Cover and interior design by H.O.T. Graphic Services

Printed in the United States of America

*To Brigette, my wife and life partner, whose encouraging nudges of confidence inspired me to believe I could one day write a book.*

# CONTENTS

# INTRODUCTION

Good intentions + wrong audience = catastrophic consequences.

Just ask Helen Georgaklis, a churchgoing real estate professional. She was helping prospective clients, a couple from her church, who needed to refinance their home.

Helen introduced them to a colleague at a financial firm where she formerly worked. How? Via e-mail, of course. Standard protocol. Simple enough.

Except for one minor problem. The colleague must have had his eye on her, because he quickly followed up on the open door her welcome e-mail provided. After addressing the business issue, he took the opportunity to add how good-looking he thought she was. "Thank you, sexy Helen," he volunteered, mentioning that he was confident all her male clients loved working with her "because you are so hot." Helen was no doubt taken aback—and doubly so the instant she noticed that the man who expressed his thoughts in an open e-mail ... had hit the *Reply All* button without thinking!

Helen's clients were so put off they began shunning her at church. Though the colleague profusely apologized to all parties, the damage was done. Epic fail.[1]

I'm guessing you can relate to the *Reply All* disaster, though I'm hoping it was less embarrassing than that. It's one thing when inappropriate, flirtatious comments get misdirected. It's another matter entirely when we believers get off message in fulfilling the Great Commission.

This book is about the tricky subject of good intentions gone awry. To be sure, our messages often come from good places in our hearts:

- "I want to please the Lord and do what He commands."
- "I want to speak the truth when a fellow believer makes a mistake ... and possibly leads others astray."
- "I want to help sinners live a much happier and healthier life than they are right now."
- "I want to make sure everyone, sinners and saints, understands what the Good Book says."

On the surface, what could possibly be wrong with such motives? Apparently, not much. Which must be why believers seem to be working overtime at standing up and sounding off.

But what if God's Word has unmistakable direction to the contrary? What if we've been missing a heavenly plan that was a little more intentional than just *Reply All*? The New Testament provides a playbook for believers that calls us to pivot our message depending on who's in our audience. And the results are unquestionably worth the effort.

That's where this book is heading.

§ § §

Before you turn the page, though, I must give a disclaimer, or maybe a plea: This book is not for everyone. It is 100 percent intended for readers who are already convinced that Jesus Christ is the best thing to ever happen to planet Earth.

If you wouldn't especially call yourself a Jesus-follower (a "Christian"), then I'd humbly request that you put this book down before opening chapter 1. Give it instead to a Christian you may know. Let them look at it first and then figure out a way to discuss it with you in person. I'm not sure how it ended up in your hands, but I didn't write this for you. Mainly, I wouldn't want you to be offended or confused by the material covered in the chapters ahead.

Thank you for considering this strange request. I hope you will be reading it very soon *after* someone introduces you to the great news about Jesus and God's amazing plan for your life.

1

# THE SOUND AND THE FURY

SMH.

You could hear social media's collective "Shaking My Head" groan. How in the world did it come to this? The 2016 U.S. presidential campaign felt anything *but* presidential. The contest between Hillary Clinton and Donald Trump took news outlets to new lows of gutter talk in print and on the screen. In the months leading up to Donald Trump's uncanny and historic election as America's forty-fifth president, both sides of the political aisle spent far more time lambasting the immorality of the other's candidate than addressing the country's future. Millions of voters expressed outrage that the names of more viable, ethical choices were not on the ballot. Throngs of Trump's detractors at home and abroad were bewildered. "Four, or possibly eight, years of this? Seriously? America, what were you thinking!"

Sounding off about politicians, sports figures, and celebrities is now clearly woven into the cultural fabric. For years now, ABC's late-night host Jimmy Kimmel has featured a comedy segment called "Mean Tweets," in which celebrities read, word for word, the nasty comment some Internet troll posted about them on Twitter. Between all the bleeps of vulgarities, some viewers find it downright humorous to watch. This is one segment, unfortunately, for which there will be no shortage of material any time soon.

Cyber-bullying goes well beyond trashing public figures. Any social media user is familiar with the pressure applied in not-so-subtle ways to join a cause or stake a claim on this issue or that. The threat looms constantly of being labeled a "hater"—either because we spoke out on a subject the wrong way (at least through one person's lens), or because our silence was somehow equated with endorsing the opposite camp.

Christians, of course, are not exempt from this phenomenon, either as trolls or targets.

In the wake of the 2015 terrorist attack in San Bernardino, Liberty University president Jerry Falwell Jr. made comments during a convocation service attended by thousands of students that quickly went viral on every national news outlet. Disturbed by President Obama's emphasis on gun control instead of terrorism, Falwell spoke in favor of students arming themselves. "I just wanted to take this opportunity to encourage all of you to get your permit. We offer a free course. Let's teach them a lesson if they ever show up here." His words referenced the university's free concealed-carry class.[2]

Students at another Christian institution, Wheaton College, rejected Falwell's theology and approach via "An Open Letter to Leaders in the Evangelical Community."[3] *The Chicago Tribune* took notice, of course, citing faculty and administration praise for the students' response.[4] Neither the Wheaton students nor the

Liberty president were alone, as other prominent Christians joined competing camps with supportive articles or soundbites online.

## My Own Hornet's Nest

I can smile about it now, but when President Obama was elected the first time, I experienced a minor dose of Internet backlash myself. Some Christians were making waves in their churches by voicing their disdain that he was elected. With all the liberal and socialist influences shaping his life, what might Barack Obama attempt with this newfound power? More than a few pastors were struggling to provide calming guidance during the uproar in their congregations.

In my position as a state overseer for several hundred churches, I felt compelled to provide leadership. Did I mention I was elected to my office just a few months before President Obama was elected to his? Sigh. I'm so naïve. I wrote a letter for pastors to read to their congregations the next Sunday if they felt it would help in viewing the election through the filter of Romans 13:1-4.

In hindsight, I should have been more careful to state that the document was for our network of churches only. It wasn't long before one of our constituents, with good intentions, posted my entire correspondence online. And that, as they say, was all she wrote!

My phone began ringing from concerned citizens outside our state. My gracious administrative assistant endured several colorful conversations, as in, "What the hell kind of church do you work at? I want to talk to your boss and let him know my opinion about his damn statement." Other callers wanted to know if I even worked for our organization. Did I really say what was being claimed online? People went above my head to our national leadership, which prompted a "just checking" phone call. I was embarrassed that my well-intentioned actions had caused them any grief. Meanwhile, a number of websites posted my comments, often out of context. Right-wing bloggers were upset with me, as were many of my fellow believers, most of whom I still haven't met.

But I had my supporters, too. While that was encouraging, it is just one small example of what has become reality—not just in society at large, which is somewhat understandable, but even in the church. Deep, deep in the church of Jesus Christ. There seems to be too little distinction between the way God's children process daily events and the response we see from a nonbelieving culture at large.

The world yells. Christians yell, too. Sometimes **louder**, or in ALL CAPS! The world rushes to make judgments about this week's target of choice. And so do Christians. Nonbelievers in every corner of culture show very little regard for whether they know the target or not. It certainly doesn't matter if they've ever met the target in person. They feel no obligation to understand the target's perspective before going into a tirade of criticism. If they don't think they like what they think the target may or may not have done, it's pretty simple, actually: Off come the gloves, and out goes the spew.

As painful as it is to type this sentence, it seems like the sons and daughters of God—the *light* and the *salt* of the world —have become comfortable taking the same approach. Can anyone disagree?

## Raising the Tension

In the summer of 2015, this came to a head in the wake of the United States Supreme Court's landmark decision affirming the legal validity of same-sex marriages. By a 5-4 vote in the case of *Obergefell v. Hodges*, the justices gave gay and lesbian couples and their supporters great cause for celebration. But they sent shockwaves, mixtures of disbelief, anger, and disappointment through many evangelical worship communities.

Pastors especially struggled. How do you properly minister to people in a situation like this? The topic certainly couldn't be ignored. That week and for the rest of the summer, this was THE talk of the nation. On TV, in print, plastered all over social media, and in daily conversations, the situation blew up. Many believers voiced their genuine anger and frustration in less than productive ways. Others, though brokenhearted, tried to be a calming influence. To many seasoned churchgoers, it resembled the heaviness they felt in the wake of *Roe v. Wade* back in 1973.

Sermon series in churches across the nation were abruptly interrupted so pastors could equip their people with a timely response. There was no choice but to provide godly counsel, and quick! *What does this mean for our country? How do you properly process your frustration? Will our church have to start hosting weddings like this? How do we explain this to our children?*

Many pastors had to do a delicate dance in light of their church's relatively recent willingness to welcome openly gay individuals to attend worship services. Closeted gays had been attending for years in many cases—seated in the same pew with closeted adulterers, hidden addicts, and private fornicators, many of whom were not only attendees but church workers and leaders and Sunday school teachers.

But this was different. Gays and lesbians had become much more public about their choices. To many evangelicals, it now seemed they wore their sexual orientation as a badge of honor. Unlike most other guests coming through the doors of welcoming churches, many gay couples looked like, and wanted to look like, well, gay couples. It had taken years for the majority of congregations to navigate their approach to reaching these men and women with the love of Christ. More and more had understood that it was possible to show Christlike fellowship without condoning lifestyles in conflict with God's Word. That was no easy task and did not happen overnight. But progress was being made.

And now, it was suddenly all in jeopardy. How do you affirm your genuine love for people who've begun to trust you … when this morning's message will make clear your conviction that their worldview is out of line with God's will for humanity? Pastors had to reinforce scriptural truths in direct opposition to the milestone legal decision some attendees that day were actually celebrating. I'm not intending to cast a judgment or pronounce all pastors who responded right or wrong with this summary. I'm just recalling the very real dilemma many pastors and Christian leaders found themselves navigating that Sunday.

And what if Sister Barnes yells *Amen!* at the wrong time? Lord, please not today!

I will never forget watching how some pastors rose to the occasion. With just two days to prepare, they put together masterful sermons with insightful resources. They prayed. Oh, how they prayed! They showed sensitivity to the makeup and culture of their local congregations, while holding faithful to the Scriptures.

Unquestionably, some took gentler approaches while others leaned toward the hard line. But God helped pastors of churches across the nation explain the context of Scripture from both the Old and New Testaments. Saints were encouraged to live holy lives, now more than ever. Citizens were informed on what the court decision did and did not mean. Myths and rumors were debunked. And on the whole, many people who love Jesus but feel same-sex attractions expressed thanks to their pastors instead of storming out in anger.

In the recently planted church where my family and I worship, our young pastor devoted three weeks to the topic. He wanted to make sure he covered things carefully, with clarity and love. On one of those weeks, there was no music or announcements. (I don't recall, but I'm betting we still took an offering.) He needed all the time he could get to walk us through the subject, literally, from Genesis to Revelation.

And it worked! Very few, if any, stood up and walked out. God was exalted. Righteousness was held high. People saw the heart and master plan of a loving Creator who has only good intentions for men and women. And the church has grown substantially since then, with frequent salvations and water baptisms.

## Foaming and Fuming

That whole phenomenon got me thinking. While I saw bright spots on the Christian landscape, I also saw reactions that made me sad and mad. Mostly sad, I think. Are we, as believers, destined to be helpless or, worse, held hostage to the daily whims of a culture that blows back and forth? Our general approach, it seems, is to wake up each day, check our Twitter feed, then figure out if we are in favor or against. Then, of course, we need to let everyone know where we stand. A few hours later, we go to sleep and start the process all over again the next day. Instead of leading culture, it feels like the present pace gives us no choice but to react. But it's not just a casual response.

Too often we have become comfortable in the role of armchair quarterback. A really loud and annoying one. And one that's not very helpful. In fact, in many cases, it seems believers are okay with stirring the pot and creating strife, not only in culture but with one another.

Navigating this climate, I sensed God's Spirit stirring something in my heart. To my own detriment, at times (and to the frustration of others), I'm the type who leans toward believing that anything is possible. Have I mentioned yet that I can be a little naïve? I kept observing the daily onslaught of division and contrary opinions, especially among believers. While I felt a lack of clarity about a specific remedy, I had no such confusion about two foundational realities. (1) This messy messaging employed by Christians that seems so random and divisive, and yet so commonplace and accepted, cannot be pleasing to the Lord. (2) Further, whatever the answer is, God has a way. No matter how challenging it may seem, God always has a way!

> **The messy messaging employed by many Christians today cannot be pleasing to the Lord.**

Before long, I stumbled on another slice of this conflict in, of all places, Ohio's serene and beautiful Amish Country. A visit there just isn't complete without enjoying at least one of the many amazing buffets to choose from. After starting a conversation with a pleasant senior citizen in line, I sat down with my wife to enjoy my mashed potatoes with buttered noodles cradled on top as God intended, instead of gravy. Within a few moments, a retired minister named Jack sauntered over to our table and introduced himself. He said his wife had met me in line and told him I was also a minister.

With tears in his eyes, Jack soon asked me if I would pray for his beloved United Methodist Church. This was a few weeks after the Supreme Court's decision, and Jack told me his church was considering a shift at their next national conference, slated for May 2016 in Portland, Oregon. "They're going to consider changing our stance on opposition to homosexuality and gay marriage," he reported. He was distraught over the possibility that the decision could allow local churches to start sanctioning wedding ceremonies for gay couples.

"But that's not all," Jack lamented. "They're also going to debate whether or not our preachers can keep their credentials even if they are practicing homosexuals." Wiping tears away, Jack added, "Ministers like me are just heartbroken. We can't believe the church we love has come to this." In light of the recent federal approval, things were not looking positive. Especially since the Episcopal Church, the Presbyterian Church (USA), and the Evangelical Lutheran Church in America had already made moves in this direction.

As I nodded in sympathy, I wasn't entirely convinced that this nice gentleman had his details down accurately. Not the

United Methodist Church! Tens of millions of believers have, no doubt, been brought into the Kingdom over the centuries as a result of Methodist preachers. They love the Word of God and have been some of its biggest proponents and defenders.

When I returned home and researched the UMC website, I discovered to my disappointment that the minister knew exactly what he was talking about. Jack, it seems, *did* know jack. Although I had missed it until that point, this effort was real, and the ensuing debate had caught the attention of all the national news outlets.

And Christians were speaking up—inside the UMC and out. People who claimed to love the same Savior were reaching dissimilar conclusions about the intent of Scripture. The debates were heated, and the world got to watch it all. CNN broadcast the news that, on the eve of the Portland meeting, 111 Methodist *pastors, deacons, elders and candidates for ministry* had taken a position online against their church's traditional stance. They "came out as lesbian, gay or bisexual ... defying their church's ban on 'self-avowed practicing homosexuals' serving in ministry and essentially daring their supervisors to discipline them."[5]

Subsequently, by a narrow margin, the quadrennial General Conference tabled the matter so a special commission could do further study and make amended recommendations. Meanwhile, believers inside and outside the UMC continue to criticize each other and their doctrine in view of the larger world.

## To Speak or Not to Speak: That Is the Question

Reading the New Testament in light of the whiplash modern-day Christians were experiencing, I went searching for clues. This is a good spot to reiterate that I'm not writing this book for "the world." I'm not even writing this for nominal churchgoers who are dubious about the claims of Scripture. I'm writing for believers like me who are convinced that, whatever the dilemma, God's Word is still God's Word. It has the answers we desperately need.

Does God's Word have anything to say about Christians with disagreements? Yes, indeed. But what is the unifying theme? Those who think Christians ought to remain quiet and live at peace have their favorite verses. Those who take the opposite approach will quote a few others.

And what about differences of opinion with the outside world? I know really solid believers who speak out about all kinds of moral issues. Some seem to enjoy debates with Christians and non-Christians alike, especially about faith and politics. Yet, I know other believers who just roll their eyes, wishing pushy, loudmouth saints would show a little more discretion. Okay, a lot more discretion. Why can't they just be quiet and let their actions do the preaching for them?

In all honesty, I have to admit I see both sides. Very often, it depends on the circumstance. Sometimes I find myself cheering on the Christian who *let 'em have it!* And then, in other situations, I want to throw something at the TV. "Shut up! You are such a lousy testimony as a follower of Christ!"

So, is that it? Is the answer simply that we each have to make our own judgment calls, case by case?

Argh! If so, then there really is no hope for greater unity in Christ's body. We all have our personal lenses and filters. Surely there has to be a more unifying principle for God's people to employ.

> **Is the answer simply that we each have to make our own judgment calls, case by case? Argh!**

Because stories like these will keep coming. An example: Pastor and televangelist Creflo Dollar has a worldwide following, appearing at conferences alongside such prominent Christian preachers as T.D. Jakes, Joel Osteen, and many others.[6] In 2015, *ABC News*[7], *CNN*[8] and others spotlighted his newest fundraising video. According to the *Atlanta Journal-Constitution*, church members and followers were being asked to "help televangelist Creflo Dollar raise the $65 million needed to buy a new private jet."[9] His former jet, more than thirty years old, was no longer usable, and his demanding schedule was said to prohibit travel by bus or commercial flights. The formula? If 200,000 people would each give $300, the needed funds would be raised. *CBS News* was one of many sources picking up the story and running with it. They featured Christians expressing support for the fundraising effort as well as those with great disdain for Pastor Dollar's approach.[10]

On a much different front: Consider the current high-profile Pope. More than any in recent memory, Pope Francis seems to have captured the fancy of a watching world, and a watching Christian community. Well, what is he? Is he liberal? Or is he conservative?

In the summer of 2016, *The New York Times* reported concerns raised by several critics of the Pope's remarks about gender identity at a private meeting with bishops in Poland.

Transcripts of the meeting later released by the Vatican capture some of the pontiff's views on the matter:

> We are experiencing a moment of the annihilation of man as the image of God. I would like to conclude with this aspect, since behind all this there are ideologies. In Europe, America, Latin America, Africa, and in some countries of Asia, there are genuine forms of ideological colonization taking place. And one of these—I will call it clearly by its name—is [the ideology of] "gender." Today children— children!—are taught in school that everyone can choose his or her sex. Why are they teaching this? Because the books are provided by the persons and institutions that give you money. These forms of ideological colonization are also supported by influential countries. And this [is] terrible!

LGBT representatives were quick to pounce, referring to the Pope's "dangerous ignorance" on the subject.[11] But many evangelicals would say the Pope was entirely justified in his concerns.

Not so much, though, when he makes more progressive comments on the environment or immigration. In a relatively short amount of time, every news outlet has ample quotations to cite (and they do so!) from prominent Christian leaders publicly expressing their disagreement with the Pope's proclamations.

Welcome to the new normal. It is what it is. And many self-described Christ-followers say we must simply accept this as the way it will be. So let's keep chanting "*Maranatha*" ("Come, Lord!") and hope for the best in the meantime. Heaven, after all, is going to be awesome! We'll forget about all this chaos one day. For now, though, there's not much we can do but cross our fingers and wait.

Really?

GET THE **MESSAGE?**

Through ever-expanding modes of communication, culture shows relatively little regard for holding back on divisive or hurtful comments.

Believers too often join in the critical fray, informing one another and the world of their frequent disappointment with immoral heathens as well as high profile saints.

God cannot be pleased with random and divisive messaging by His children; those who plant their faith in His Word believe He always has a better way.

Meanwhile, the plethora of preferred means and theology employed by Christians in determining how to express their varied opinions and perspectives shows few signs of cohesion.

# "NEW TESTAMENT NORMAL"

If a fellow believer strongly disagrees with you or with me, does that automatically mean one of us is in sin?

Not necessarily. For example, don't you know solid believers who feel differently about boycotting Disney? I sure do! How about immigration? Some Christ-followers think we should show more compassion toward undocumented immigrants. Others who are no doubt on their way to heaven firmly disagree. They believe we have to severely strengthen our borders in order to preserve the union. Both camps might agree on being pro-life and pro-guns, but they are miles apart on immigration. They both love God's Word and believe we should make choices today based on biblical principles.

On many issues, onlookers might wonder whether we are all reading the same Bible. We sometimes joke about the sibling who charted their own unique path, saying, "Were they raised by the same parents I was?" It often feels that way with spiritual brothers and sisters. "Are they reading the same Scripture I am?"

Admittedly, no one has seen the lips of Jesus moving for nearly twenty centuries. It's been equally as long since anyone heard sounds coming from the mouths of the first apostles such as Peter and Paul. Those sounds, and subsequently their pens, formed words and sentences … but that was then. How do believers today, far removed from those live interactions, have any confidence that our own words and actions are consistent with the intentions of Scripture? Especially on matters where we disagree with fellow believers, or even with the world.

Members of the same family living together day in and day out find the task of catching the intent a constant and sizable challenge. Eager, good-hearted husbands often mistake their wives' statement "I had such a rough day" as a direct invitation to help fix the problem. Or better yet, to fix the problem people who messed with them. Instead, on that particular evening, after the last kid has gone to bed, the message is a simple request to just listen for a few minutes. What she is really saying is *Could you please offer a little empathy? Nothing more. I just need to know that someone understands how crazy my day was.*

Now when it comes to catching the hints and subtleties of Scripture, that gap gets even larger. The Bible, to many, seems ancient. For others, it's so complex, it's so deep, it's so big, it's so boring, it's so irrelevant, it's so violent. How can we possibly understand it, much less be confident that we are applying the good parts as intended? Perhaps there are general applications, but do Bible enthusiasts actually believe we can make solid life decisions today based on the writings of well-meaning authors who never heard about global terrorism, climate change or the Internet?

In fact, aren't there many stories and examples throughout the Bible that were never meant, even thousands of years ago, to serve as guidelines for good, healthy living? Surely no reader is expected to excel in acts of betrayal and suicide simply because Judas was a disciple and that's what he did. How can we know for sure which characters are positive role models and which ones aren't? Don't Christians believe and teach, for example, that the apostle Peter made some really sad, inappropriate choices along with some very wise and impactful ones?

It follows, then, that there might be some examples in Scripture of believers disagreeing, but perhaps the lesson is for us to learn how *not* to do it. How can we know for sure?

Further, don't we need to apply a time-and-culture filter? Christ's instruction to shake off the dust from our feet when we leave an unreceptive village comes to mind. Taken literally, that doesn't seem very applicable for most missionaries, who now tend to wear shoes instead of going barefoot or sporting sandals. We tend to get from place to place on asphalt, using bicycles, cars, and planes.

There are, of course, many locales where dusty roads are still the norm. But the greater symbolism of this exercise, beyond its literal application, holds value in any context, even when our message is rejected online.

## Donkeys and Reptiles and Whales—Oh, My!

The consequences of literalism can be, quite literally, deadly. *USA Today* reported on the February 2014 death of Pastor Jamie Coots from Kentucky, known by viewers of the *National Geographic Channel's* reality show *Snake Salvation*.[12] His death from a rattlesnake bite during church followed the similar 2012 demise of Pastor Mark Wolford of West Virginia, as reported by the *Washington Post*.[13]

Proponents of religious snake-handling often cite one solitary New Testament instruction and one New Testament experience to support what they do. They remind anyone who will listen that Jesus told His disciples (and us) that they would "take up serpents" as part of fulfilling the Great Commission (Mark 16:18). Later, the apostle Paul himself was bitten by a poisonous snake and miraculously survived (Acts 28:1-6). Voila! There's the "proof."

The vast majority of Christian leaders today reject that theology. Paul's is the only recorded case of a poisonous snakebite in the New Testament. He had not awakened that morning hoping for such an encounter. Paul had no idea the snake was nearby when it slithered out of a brush pile and latched onto his hand. This incident, apparently, was exhibit A of Christ's message in Mark 16. The larger point for all believers is that, whether an attack comes from a snakebite, or lethal poisons from toxic food or beverage, we should believe for divine protection when encountering physical threats while spreading the gospel. There was no intent in the Lord's instruction, nor have any Bible scholars ever cited New Testament examples, of believers *intentionally* picking up snakes to demonstrate their obedience or prove a point.

While handling poisonous snakes in church is a rather extreme example, it helps us grasp the lesson about the dangers of taking a single verse out of context. Presbyterians and Pentecostals agree on this. So do Mennonites and Methodists. We don't take a single verse about Paul's encounter with a snake and turn it into routine, encouraged practice.

Similarly, we wouldn't want to take a single verse or story about confronting a nonbeliever and apply it in a way it was never intended. New Testament exchanges between Jesus and the Samaritan woman, John the Baptist and Herod, and Paul the apostle and Felix the governor are all examples we will review with this in mind. As we focus on the biblical model of communication in the chapters ahead, we really can train ourselves to hear the approaching hiss before someone accidentally gets poisoned by our words.

Further illuminating this principle are a few animal stories from the Old Testament. Good, godly things happened to prophets because of supernaturally-enabled animals. Balaam was a prophet who received timely counsel from a talking donkey. The prophet Elijah's life was saved by ravens proficient in fast-food delivery. Jonah's legacy as the prophet who led the largest revival in the Bible has been credited to a fish chauffeur.

While some may doubt these incidents, most Christian leaders and millions more followers affirm their belief that these supernatural encounters with animals actually happened. Yet few, if any, carry over that belief into literal practice or common expectations. When seeking God's direction for our lives, believers are seldom encouraged by their pastors to start looking for talking donkeys. Instead, the vehicles of prayer and Bible study are recommended. Hungry Christians are not instructed to hold out their arms so bagel-bearing ravens have an inviting place to land. Most have adopted more practical remedies, like getting a job. Missionaries typically take planes to their overseas assignments rather than wading into the ocean with their suitcases and children so a whale can swallow them whole.

Do most Christians then reject the notion that Balaam actually changed course and headed the right direction because his donkey spoke human words he could understand and told him to go a different way? When Elijah was hiding from King Ahab in a remote ravine, was he being lazy or disobedient to only eat bread and meat delivered twice a day by ravens instead of wandering out on his own to hunt for food? Should Jonah have hopped right back in a boat and headed home when the great fish vomited him up on the shore en route to Nineveh? Most evangelicals quickly say, "No." All three prophets responded positively after encountering the animals.

Apparently, then, Christians today routinely read about good, God-ordained encounters in the Bible that they choose *not* to adopt for their own lives. Yet at the same time, they feel downright adamant about other such encounters in Scripture that *must* be adopted—not only by themselves but by others, too, to the point that refusing to do so amounts to sinful rebellion. So by what principles do Christians make such determinations? On what basis do they say that some legitimately authentic and positive examples thousands of years ago were not meant to be repeated today, while others are? This far into the twenty-first century, how can we have confidence that we are handling our communication the way God wants us to?

## Looking for Patterns

We look for two complementary patterns in God's Word, especially in the New Testament: *patterns of instruction*, paired with *patterns of experience*. What principles for Christian living are repeated by numerous teachers and authors in the Bible to numerous audiences? And, which of those teachings are further supported by repeated stories of esteemed believers who experienced or demonstrated them? In other words, they practiced what they preached while also preaching what they practiced.

This is what I call *New Testament Normal*. Geographical, social, and cultural differences aside, what God-honoring behaviors by the early disciples should all Christians in all cultures consider normative, routine, and expected? If such patterns actually exist regarding our messaging, wouldn't we all want to carefully explore them?

Patterns like this are unquestionably paramount to all we do as believers. An obvious example: Jesus repeatedly highlighted the value of prayer to His disciples. Paul later encouraged his readers (as did Peter, James, and John in their writings) to do the same thing. That frequency causes Christians today to notice a *pattern of instruction* in the New Testament. We conclude that believers ought to pray to their heavenly Father on a regular basis.

Further, we read in other chapters and other accounts by other authors that Jesus made a habit of praying Himself. He often took His disciples with Him to pray. After Jesus ascended to heaven, the pattern continued. Believers such as Peter and John in the book of Acts (and in numerous other New Testament books) prayed on a frequent basis. Hence, modern-day Christ-followers embrace this *pattern of experience* in God's Word with zero pushback.

Believers in the Bible were repeatedly instructed to pray, and believers in the Bible repeatedly experienced prayer. This tandem evidence of instruction and experience has given Christians throughout the centuries the unwavering confidence that prayer is to be employed with rigor, even today. Prayer was normal then; prayer should be normal now.

Other examples: The *act of worship*, which gets repeated instruction and repeated illustration. *Sharing the gospel* is supported by both patterns. So is *giving generously* of our financial resources to the work of the local church and to missions. Hundreds of millions of believers today, across national, cultural, racial, generational, and even denominational lines, reach largely similar conclusions about expected Christian behavior based on repeated patterns of instruction and experience in the New Testament. "My suggestion would be that one looks for positive repeated patterns in the text," writes theologian Ben Witherington III. "Repetition is the key clue."[14]

So what about those animals? Why don't today's preachers routinely harp on their parishioners to be on the lookout for donkeys that speak, ravens that cook, and whales that taxi? Because there is no pattern of instruction nor pattern of experience to support such teachings. Only one donkey in the Bible spoke. Only one flock of ravens brought food. Only one fish carried a prophet in its belly for three days. Apparently, Christians have concluded that there is no expectation for, nor is there benefit from, intentionally pursuing these specific types of encounters with the animal kingdom. For the child of God, that's not normal.

Instead, it should be normal for us to follow scriptural directives that are based on repeated instruction plus experience. This is not to say that abnormal interventions don't happen from time to time. Throughout the Bible, we see God speaking to and moving among His children in individually unique ways. I certainly believe that God has revealed His nature to me personally and powerfully—especially during a time as a young father when I battled cancer. Decades later, I can vividly recall the specific clues and confirmation I felt God gave to me in a very personal manner during that trying season. In one instance, when I wrestled with the real possibility of perishing, God graciously brought me all the way back in my mind to a Sunday school lesson when I was in kindergarten. I was incredibly comforted that day when I vividly remembered what the teacher, Louise, had revealed from Ephesians 6 about honoring our parents, so we could *live long on the earth.*

Christians can and should deeply value all the ways God speaks and interacts with them personally. But we do so while avoiding the temptation to pressure other believers to experience God in the same way we did. This is all the more important when abnormal components not bolstered by the pattern of New Testament instruction and experience are involved.

### How Shall We Then Talk?

Is there, then, any reliable pattern of instruction in Scripture about our speech, especially in the New Testament? Are there patterns on what should be our normal conversation in this culture, during these exceptional times of disunity and unrest? And, if there are, is there also a recognizable pattern of experience to support such instruction?

Specifically, can we find abundant New Testament support for Christians ridiculing other Christians? Because that seems pretty normal nowadays—calling out other believers with whom we have no relationship whatsoever, having never approached them privately about our concerns before letting them have it publicly. Publicly, that is, not only in front of other believers but even in full view of unbelievers. Is this the New

Testament way to let them know what we (and God) think they did wrong?

Based on what we routinely observe and practice in our time, is it also true that the New Testament condones regularly confronting and arguing with nonbelievers about their moral choices? Do we see apostles such as Paul and Peter challenging pagans in the name of Jesus about their politics, their sexual habits, and the harmful substances they consume?

Well, of course, there are no such patterns of instruction—or patterns of experience. Instead, there is a crystal-clear (and refreshing!) pattern for normal communication woven throughout the New Testament that shines the way for believers in this and every century. It's a New Testament Normal (NTN) set of audience guidelines that robustly incorporate that beautiful, freeing, powerful, and confidence-instilling partnership of instruction and experience. It is abundant. And strikingly, it is without exception.

God clearly advocates understanding who our audience is. This is not at all in conflict with the value God places on understanding the message (His Word) or the messenger (His children) or the ultimate Author (Himself). Rather, it is an enhancement needed now more than ever. The New Testament pattern of instruction and experience about fully appreciating the importance of our audience irrefutably heightened the

> **There is a crystal-clear New Testament pattern that shines the way for believers in this and every century.**

28

effectiveness of those early church messengers and their message, while bringing immense pleasure and worship to the Author.

It leads us to ask ourselves such questions as: *Who am I talking to? Who is watching me? In the moments when my life is communicating to others, whether by word or deed, who is in my audience?*

The New Testament disciples frequently had nonbelievers within earshot, and they knew it. This led them, as God's messengers, to manage their message accordingly in a striking and consistent display of Spirit-empowered emotional intelligence.

In the numerous accounts we read, nonbelievers never observed Christians critiquing one another. Instead, they routinely saw how much they loved one another. Further, nonbelievers never heard Christians reprimanding them about moral or political issues, because the key message for them stayed focused like a laser on preaching Christ crucified.

The remainder of this book will take a deep dive into the New Testament in an effort to show the prevalence and depth of these patterns.

Some believers today swallow these conclusions without flinching, almost yawning. It simply mirrors what they have felt and how they have managed their own message, whether or not they have ever expressed it that directly. Others find one or more of those assertions highly, or at least partially, objectionable. This is the camp into which I fell. After all, I said to myself, are we really supposed to sit tight and say nothing when believers who should know better are behaving in a manner inconsistent with what Scripture teaches? Drunkenness leads to all kinds of pain and misery, in this life and the next, so does the Bible imply Christians shouldn't care that a nonbeliever is ruining her life and the lives of those she loves? Is this another attempt to lay guilt on Christians because some may be offended by the truth they speak about gay marriage?

Regardless of whether you embrace or reject these claims, I'm convinced the probability for many believers is high, as it was for me, that we haven't previously considered this, at least not thoroughly. What role did audience play in what was New Testament Normal (NTN) for communication by Christ's disciples?

In the midst of hostile and perilous times, a repeated pattern of instruction and experience emerged in relation to who was in the audience. I hope this discovery will inspire you and give you confidence. Yes, believers *are* intended to be on the same page! We *are* designed to operate from a much greater sense of peace and clarity so we don't get caught up in the nervousness and unsettled chatter swirling around us. Ultimately, I pray this investment of yours will produce far greater results in your life, your church, and your world—the kind of results that were also NTN, as they powerfully built up other believers and drew scores of nonbelievers into the family of God.

# GET THE
# MESSAGE?

Ardent Christ-followers throughout the ages are able to operate with relative confidence that they are interpreting Scripture's intentions as God desires.

Instead of using one or two biblical phrases or random stories out of context, believers apply the Bible's themes through the lens of positive patterns of instruction which are bolstered by positive patterns of experience.

Throughout the New Testament, positive patterns of instruction (teaching) and experience (practice) include widely embraced approaches toward frequent prayer, worship, Bible study, and evangelization, all of which appeared to be NTN (New Testament Normal).

For too long, it has become commonplace for believers and even Christian leaders to engage in communication in direct contrast to NTN patterns regarding our audience of nonbelievers. These include speaking ill of fellow believers in front of nonbelievers and pressuring nonbelievers over non-gospel issues, such as immoral choices and political preferences.

3

# PUBLIC SPATS

She said *what?*

No, she didn't!

Well, yes, she did, actually. The Internet was buzzing in the summer of 2014 with news that one of America's popular Christian voices had made a seemingly off-base statement from her pulpit. While speaking at the world-renowned megachurch in Houston that she and her husband, Joel Osteen, have pastored for years, she said, "When you come to church, when you worship Him, you're not doing it for God really. You're doing it for yourself, because that's what makes God happy. Amen?" Hmmm. Really?

Her words were of course heard and seen on nationwide television, which is how a 36-second clip quickly showed up on YouTube. Victoria Osteen had been criticized before, but the repudiations this time came fast and sharp. How could any pastor tell congregants that worship is actually for personal benefit and not for God? "I could just puke," posted one observer.[15]

To her credit, Osteen later released a statement acknowledging that she "could have been more articulate" in her remarks, and that she did not "mean to imply that we don't worship God; that's ridiculous."[16] But the damage had been done. One secular news outlet reported, "Once the video began making rounds on social media, many in the Christian community took to Twitter and personal blogs to express their dismay at Osteen's comments."[17] Her hometown newspaper ran with the headline "Christians Berate Victoria Osteen's Cheap Christianity."[18]

A much different kind of preacher caught public flak a few years earlier when he agreed to give the invocation at newly elected President Barack Obama's 2008 inauguration. Rick Warren of Saddleback Church in southern California was on record for defining marriage as a covenant between a man and a woman. He had even supported California's successful Proposition 8 to that effect. So what was he doing now cozying up to this pro-choice, gay-friendly president? LGBT activists and various political figures were apoplectic that Warren, of all people, had been selected.

But Warren also received criticism from those inside the church. News outlets such as *The Wall Street Journal* carried stories with quotes from various Christian leaders who voiced their disapproval.[19] How could an evangelical pastor do anything that could be interpreted as supporting this kind of president? "God will deal with you on this ... God will not wink at this," a fellow member of Warren's denomination thundered in a widely circulated e-mail. "I pray He is kind to you in this punishment that is coming."[20]

## How Would Jesus Confront?

I'm not seeking in this chapter to render a verdict on either one of these dust-ups. The issue here is not about whether or not Rick Warren should have accepted or declined the invitation. Did Victoria Osteen really mean what she said? I am inclined to believe her follow-up statement, as I think most preachers would. In the midst of a sermon, haven't we all said things that came out differently than what we intended!

But how many of the Christians who took to Twitter and personal blogs had first reached out privately to Warren or Osteen, or to their respective church boards, for clarification? Smartphones and Twitter accounts aside, what patterns of instruction and experience does the New Testament give for handling a believer whose words seem a little off? Do the Gospels or Epistles include directives on berating one another in public? Do we read accounts about serious conflict among believers in the New Testament?

Actually, yes. If anything was normal about life for the early church, it was the challenge to assimilate new converts and their peculiar ideas. Conflict was normal, but so was joy. Gaining new converts and growing the saints was invigorating. It was also exhausting. Motivating. Stretching. Rewarding. And unrelenting. This is why a careful review of NTN disciplines is so warranted. Watch how particularly true this is when it comes to confronting other believers.

Jesus is only recorded as having used the actual word "church" (*ecclesia* in Greek, literally, an assembly) in two settings. The first was in a conversation with His disciple Peter, when He uttered the oft-quoted words "I will build My church, and the gates of Hades shall not prevail against it" (Matt. 16:18). The second, in Matthew 18, was a longer exposition on something the corporate church would do. Of all the activities our Lord could have addressed—evangelism, worship, education, finances, you name it—He specifically wanted to talk about how the assembly of believers in a particular locale should lovingly hold misbehaving members accountable.

This directive is noteworthy due to its timing. Though the people of God already shared a worshipful community in the Jewish context, the New Testament church as we know it had not even yet been born. Jesus had not yet suffered, died, resurrected, or ascended to heaven. Much more about the church and its mission comes to light following the Holy Spirit's arrival at Pentecost. But here, Jesus was preparing the disciples—those in whom He was entrusting the very launch of the church worldwide—with the understanding that corporate accountability and confrontation *inside the church* is non-negotiable for the most important mission in history.

He gave a clear, step-by-step explanation of how to proceed:

> "Moreover if your brother sins against you, go and tell him his fault between you and him alone. If he hears you, you have gained your brother. But if he will not hear, take with you one or two more, that 'by the mouth of two or three witnesses every word may be established.' And if he refuses to hear them, tell it to the church. But if he refuses even to hear the church, let him be to you like a heathen and a tax collector.
>
> "Assuredly, I say to you, whatever you bind on earth will be bound in heaven, and whatever you loose on earth will be loosed in heaven.

"Again I say to you that if two of you agree on earth concerning anything that they ask, it will be done for them by My Father in heaven. For where two or three are gathered together in My name, I am there in the midst of them." (Matthew 18:15-20 NKJV)

Apparently, it is NTN for Christian confrontation to happen in stages, *inside* the church. What all does this assume? Several things.

- This particular passage addresses sinful offenses *previously* committed against us *personally*. (By contrast, note that Jesus did not hesitate to confront Peter in front of the immediate crowd when he was wielding his sword at the high priest's servant; see Matthew 26:52-54.)
- Though there is incredible wisdom here for a variety of imaginable conflict scenarios, the prescription Jesus provides for when "your brother sins" implies that both parties are believers.
- Further, we're not talking about blatant criminal behavior. In the case of child molestation or child abuse, for example, at least part of the appropriate response may include alerting the civil authorities. (It is most ideal, of course, when the offending party comes to terms with their own need to self-report, take ownership, and ask for forgiveness.)
- It is also fair to discern that Jesus isn't focusing His remarks on the tendency of some people to overreact at the slightest offense. To be easily offended is not one

of the spiritual gifts! Many things people say and do should, in fact, be overlooked, especially if the tension is not about blatant sin but about preferences or even a serious difference of opinion. (Is this a good time to talk about the selection of songs for church worship services?)

- Since Christ is talking about believers only, we can also assume that all sides should desire a resolution that will bring glory to God. The passage concludes with a reminder that Christ is in the midst of us. Whether the resolution comes quickly or not, we can pray together and expect that God will show His children the way forward, even when the issues seem heavy.

Now to the particulars of what Jesus prescribed:

## First Stage: One-to-One

When a definite offense erupts, we might first ask ourselves: Have we thought and prayed over the matter? Have we considered the situation in the eyes of multiple Bible passages? If so, and if it still seems like what was done or said was a clear violation of Christian principles, and that sin has occurred, the counsel in Matthew 18 (and throughout the New Testament) gives clarity for the Christian's response. *Go directly to the person. Talk to her. Explain to him (or them, if there were several offenders) in private—one Jesus-follower to another—why you feel what happened (or didn't happen) needs to be addressed and resolved.*

We don't need to automatically bother the pastor (or the pastor's spouse) with the news. At least, not yet. As we will explore, the benefits of this private approach can be incredibly life-giving.

Jesus addressed this challenging subject in another conversation, again setting the stage for one-on-one dialog. When someone keeps offending you, He said in Luke 17:3-4, go directly to that person. Rebuke them, then forgive them. In fact, keep forgiving them even if they go on wronging you and then asking for forgiveness.

Paul reinforced this concept with the instruction to gently and humbly restore a brother or sister who is sinning (Gal. 6:1ff). Even the one who claims to be part of a church but causes division by promoting heresy gets the "stages" treatment (see Titus 3:10). All of this, while we take care not to speak badly about our brothers and sisters (James 4:11) or grumble against one another (James 5:9).

## Second Stage: Duo (or Trio) to One

But what if the first stage doesn't succeed? For good reason, there is a limit—for the offender's sake, for your sake, for the church's sake, and, equally important, for the world's sake.

When it becomes clear that sincere repentance is not in the offender's plans, offendees are not helpless. At this point, Christ says to bring another trusted Christian or two into the mix. They don't have to get overly involved. In fact, they don't have to say a word. Their role is not to serve on the judge's bench, but in the witness stand a few important feet away. This is not about judging the offender as right or wrong, yet.

The genius of this tactic is that, if there really is an offense here, the offender will many times hop voluntarily onto the judge's seat, drop the gavel on himself, and start repenting.

All the third party had to do was to be in the room, on the phone call, or part of the video chat. (Have you noticed how much better conversations go when they can benefit, unlike e-mail, from tone, inflection, and body language?) If needed later, there is now reputable testimony as to whether or not the confrontation happened, when and how it happened, in a manner consistent with Scripture.

How kind and gracious of our loving Creator to grab our attention like this, before it is too late, before we cause more long-lasting and inappropriate pain in another believer's life. He wants to see us forgiven and walking in harmony with Him and all His children. He wants us to learn so we will know how to handle things when someone offends us down the road. He intends for the church to be as healthy as it can be. Before everyone else in the church finds out, before our heart gets so entrenched in pride that we find it humanly impossible to apologize, God creates a second escape hatch with our name on it.

Is this always easy? Hardly! Admit we were wrong? Apologize to someone? Then ask for their help to avoid a repeat in the future? Often, it's tough and sometimes complicated. What if others besides us were partially at fault, too? Maybe the person who offended this time around was the one who was painfully offended in a prior situation by the very person who is now crying, "Foul!" Often the offender cannot process the situation with complete vulnerability because there is strong suspicion, or even evidence, that the confronter's motives are not entirely noble. Having the added perspective of another mature believer or two in the room often causes both parties to see a somewhat bigger, more objective picture.

In the Galatians passage mentioned earlier, Paul states it this way: "Dear brothers and sisters, if another believer is overcome by some sin, you who are godly should gently and humbly help that person back onto the right path. And be careful not to fall into the same temptation yourself. Share each other's burdens, and in this way obey the law of Christ. If you think you are too important to help someone, you are only fooling yourself. You are not that important" (Gal. 6:1-3 NLT).

### Third Stage: A Congregational Hearing

I'm guessing the third stage of Matthew 18 is altogether foreign to many modern-day believers. Have you actually seen some type of members' meeting where the offender was present for a group confrontation? As uncomfortable as it may sound, that's what Jesus prescribes. If the first two rounds of confrontation have proven ineffective, this is the last straw. (Well, more accurately, the second-to-last straw.)

In a final attempt to bring reconciliation, the offender should be offered one more opportunity, in a large-group setting, to repent. The pastor and other church leaders say, "Friend, this is your last chance. We have carefully weighed the matter. We've repeatedly prayed and checked the Scriptures. We've verified sources. And we firmly conclude that a serious offense has occurred.

"Now please know this: We love you and don't want to see you leave the fellowship of this church. But you must acknowledge your error, ask for forgiveness, and turn from this type of behavior."

Thankfully, this heightened drama is rarely experienced because reconciliation happened in earlier stages. The plan

Jesus laid out really works much of the time! It should be clear from reading this passage that heaven's goal is for resolution prior to the need for a tactic this public.

But sometimes, an unrepentant offender will choose to pass on this final opportunity, deeming it wrong-headed or too intimidating. Many believers are also unfamiliar with this part of the process because the offended party, or even the church leaders, chickened out. "On second thought, you know what? Maybe we can handle this in a more discreet way." This short-term dodge can sadly be followed by long-term confusion. "Why does everyone seem to be treating her differently than they used to?" Or, "I wonder why we never see him around here anymore."

The third stage can work. I've seen it with my own eyes. After several previous attempts to produce positive change, the sobriety of having the entire congregation aware of what happened can catch an offender's attention. *Do I really want to lose out on all this love, all these friendships, all this support ... simply because I can't lower my pride to admit I messed up?*

Such a confrontation is also incredibly preventative in nature. Not only will the offender likely think twice before committing a repeat offense, but so will all the witnesses. Wouldn't you? When handled appropriately by all parties, others in the church dealing with similar temptations are often encouraged by seeing the love and forgiveness of God in action.

However ...

### If All Else Fails

Only after grace upon grace does Jesus get to the final verdict of dismissing the offender from the fellowship. Romans 1 talks about God handing repeated, unrepentant sinners over to fulfill their own lusts. In 1 Corinthians 5, Paul tells his readers to do essentially the same thing when a man in the church remains in an incestuous relationship with his stepmother. For these folks' own good, in this life and in the one to come, they cannot continue to be treated as believers. Someone who insists on continuing to break God's commandments after repeated and loving confrontation by a community of believers can call themselves whatever they want: "Enlightened." "Expressing themselves." "Not that bad." The list is endless. But Scripture refuses to call them believers, and so should Christians.

So, just as it was NTN to use graduated steps in the confrontation process, it was also NTN to stop treating the person like a fellow believer if necessary. As harsh as it sounds, the motive of heaven is one of tremendous, strategic, and effective love. In all New Testament passages on this matter, the intent every time is for the spiritual separation to be temporary, not permanent.

## Loving vs. Endorsing

How is this process working out in our time?

Too often, well-intentioned believers contribute to a permanent rupture by refusing to follow this temporary but critical reset. Does removing a nonrepentant brother or sister from the fellowship of the church mean we hate them or pretend they died? Do we begin to spread rumors about them or seek to cause them harm? No. In fact, when Jesus instructs His disciples that the unrepentant believer needs to be treated ultimately like a heathen and tax collector, we need to ask ourselves what that means.

Jews, even believing Jews, kept an arm's length from Gentiles. Similarly, tax collectors were not invited to family gatherings. At the same time, did the Jesus we read about in the Gospels routinely avoid all interaction with those two groups? Does the name Zacchaeus ring a bell? Jesus was intentionally friendly with these people. Still, He did not give any nonbeliever the impression they were already forgiven and on their way to eternal life as a child of God. He did not call them "brother" or "sister" until they repented and earnestly followed Him.

So which is it? In light of the fact that Jesus is talking here about a *believer* who refuses to reconcile, after multiple attempts by the church leaders, the passage points toward a hard break. Why? Because there is a clear difference between a lifelong heathen and an unrepentant Christian. Jesus seems to be referencing the traditional Jewish treatment of heathen Gentiles rather than His amended personal approach. Like a parent laying down the law for a child he loves, to banish the disobedient believer from the church is a really tough, but really loving thing to do.

By contrast, believers who cannot bring themselves to draw a clear line and directly confront the unrepentant person are playing with fire. Though it can feel more comfortable in the short term, avoiding the sin conversation fosters an unhealthy co-existence where the guilty party reasonably concludes there must be no pressing need for change. It can be, in the end, one of the cruelest forms of enabling, because the consequences are so potentially devastating and so eternal.

If this is troubling, take heart. Good news is coming! Probably some of the best you've heard in a while. Hang in there as we wade through the tougher conversations.

While it's hard when the unrepentant church member is someone you see on Sunday mornings, the emotions, challenges, and second-guessing escalate dramatically when the offender lives under your own roof. Maybe the offense was so contentious they now live under another roof. Mixed messages from other family members and even church members, often based on kind intentions, can further complicate matters. Perhaps some overreact and stray from healthy confrontation into mean and hateful attacks. Harsh words are so hard to take back. Or, maybe one family member musters the resolve to hold the line, aiming to show tough love ... but then another loved one can't stand the pressure and caves, apologizing to the offender for how rudely all the other *so-called* Christians in the family are behaving.

Leadership and clarity on the matter are crucial. There is no New Testament example where these kinds of situations were swept under the rug. Paul is clear about naming names and offenses on numerous occasions. The entire church has to stick together if this final step of accountability is to be successful, with the gracious end goal in mind. There's no guarantee of a quick or even an eventual turnaround. The offender may, sadly, walk away forever. But the likelihood of repentance and restoration of unity in the body is greatly increased by taking this NTN approach.

I love the story of my friend Sarah. Although raised in the rural Midwest in the home of godly parents who faithfully attended a Bible-believing church, she endured unkind teasing in high school that fostered seeds of confusion and hurt. Subsequently, during college, she found herself fully embracing a lesbian lifestyle.

Her parents and family members were devastated. They knew Sarah had accepted Christ and had so much potential for living a life that would glorify her Savior. But she relocated to the West Coast to try to escape the accountability of her family and her church, ultimately falling in love with another girlfriend.

Sarah was eventually hired as a public high school teacher and became the faculty adviser for the Gay-Straight Student Alliance on campus. Engaged to be married in one of the few states where such unions were legal at the time, and now the new owners of a home, Sarah and her betrothed were very frustrated when Sarah's parents declined to participate in her wedding. They said they could not celebrate an act so clearly contrary to scriptural teaching. Instead, her parents asked, could they come out in advance of the wedding and spend some time with her and her fiancée?

Sarah acquiesced. Her mom and dad came out for the visit. They were friendly and cordial, in spite of tension in the air. One night, however, Sarah's fiancée had gone out for a few hours, leaving Sarah alone in her room. Sarah's parents were interceding for Sarah and her friend when they could hear her screaming loudly in the next room. They sensed spiritual warfare was taking place and continued praying.

As Sarah tells it now, she saw an unmistakable vision of the horribly frightening Enemy of her soul. In those moments of screaming and trembling, she was overcome with the sensation of evil forces. As soon as the evil presence subsided, Sarah went into the room where her parents were praying. In her words, "they just kept praying while I had it out with God." Several supernatural events were about to take place.

Moments later, with Sarah still in their room, her mother began speaking in tongues for the first time in her life, after years of praying to be baptized in the Holy Spirit. Sarah, meanwhile, sensed in her own spirit that God was giving her an ultimatum. She wasn't happy about it at all, but she knew God was telling her it was time to serve Him wholeheartedly and to forsake the lifestyle that was causing harm to both her and her girlfriend. To disobey, she realized, would have devastating eternal ramifications. This, of course, was another long-awaited answer to her parents' prayers.

Fast-forward to today, and Sarah continues her preparation for missionary service in Central America. Her former fiancée gave her heart to Jesus as well and married a Christian man several years ago. Sarah can't thank her parents enough for remaining steadfast in their love and kindness to her, while not yielding to the point of expressing approval of her sinful choices.

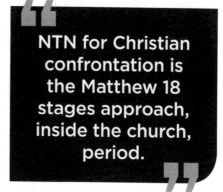

> NTN for Christian confrontation is the Matthew 18 stages approach, inside the church, period.

## Meanwhile, on the Barricades

It is an odd commentary on twenty-first-century Christians that the pattern of instruction on this type of loving but firm engagement with family members or in the house of God is so often avoided, while another form of confrontation found nowhere in Scripture is so heartily embraced. Unlike the recent anecdotes we hear about all too often, there are no New Testament examples of sinning believers who were later confronted by other believers in any public context where nonbelievers are listening. None. NTN for Christian confrontation is the Matthew 18 stages approach, inside the church, period.

Nowadays in pulpits, on websites and social media, in books and magazines, and over the mediums of radio, TV, and satellite, wherever you look, it is open season on believers—by other believers! And they're naming names. One of those names is Kentucky county clerk Kim Davis. In the wake of the 2015 United States Supreme Court decision declaring same-sex marriages legal nationwide, she became the face of Christian revolt. She made national headlines week after week when, in the face of jail time, she refused to sign marriage licenses for same-sex couples.

Blistering criticism came from expected circles in politics and media who did not share her Christian worldview on the biblical definition of marriage. They wanted her to shut up, do her job, or resign. Many Christians quickly rose to her defense, including presidential candidates Mike Huckabee and Ted Cruz.

But she was also berated by fellow Christians, many identifying themselves as conservative Christians. Fox News profiled a prominent evangelical publicly voicing his disapproval of Mrs. Davis's actions, challenging her theology, in addition to her civil duty.[21] One Florida pastor took to Facebook to dissect even her hidden motives: "This seems to be a case of someone looking to cash in on the Religious Right. Churches all across the South will throw money at her to come and tell congregations how the evil American government put her in jail because of her faith in Jesus.

"This is why we are losing.

"This is why people have such disdain for evangelicals."[22]

The point here, and throughout this chapter, has nothing to do with whether Victoria Osteen, Rick Warren, or Kim Davis was 100 percent right or 100 percent wrong in these brief episodes of their lives as believers. Whether they were completely innocent, or completely sinning, doesn't either prospect dramatically highlight the rationale for handling Christian confrontation in an NTN manner?

Instead, we seem to have adopted the Yelp method of social media reviews on our brothers and sisters. We sound off on fellow believers (often anonymously) just like we rate the hotels, restaurants, and stores we frequent. We see no need to try contacting them first, or to investigate if Christians who actually have a relationship with them are already in the process of doing so. The easy availability of computer keyboards and phones that record videos have apparently negated the need for going to the person directly and giving them several chances to consider a change in their ways. Matthew 18, make room for Yelp 24/7! If *ever* the statement "We do it simply because we can" applied!

All of this, of course, is in direct violation of the substantial NTN pattern of instruction to show respect to fellow believers. Look hard in the New Testament for the positive, exemplary case of a believer complaining about other believers in front of heathens, or airing their dirty laundry, and you simply won't find it. How have we ever become comfortable publicly criticizing brothers and sisters when faced with such a litany of commandments to the contrary? These gems, among many others, quickly ring a bell:

- Do unto others as you would have others do unto you. (Luke 6:31)
- Be devoted to one another with brotherly love; prefer one another in honor. (Romans 12:10)
- Dare any of you, having a matter against another, go to the law before the unrighteous, and not before the saints? (1 Corinthians 6:1)
- And be kind one to another, tenderhearted, forgiving one another, just as God in Christ also forgave you. (Ephesians 4:32)
- Therefore encourage one another and build each other up. (1 Thessalonians 5:1 NIV)
- If there is any encouragement in Christ, if any comfort of love, if any fellowship of the Spirit, if any compassion and mercy, then fulfill my joy and be like-minded, having the same love, being in unity with one mind. (Philippians 2:1-2)

## We Can Do Better

A holy revolt in the ranks of believers is overdue. When a believer starts a conversation about a misbehaving Christian who has not been given the benefit of NTN confrontation, why not directly, privately rebuke the source of the accusation, or at least start intentionally walking away? When a professional Christian blogger or even a casual Facebook member sounds off on some prominent believer, let's try sending them a private message encouraging them to cease and desist. We certainly can stop ourselves from contributing to or encouraging the online chat. Unless the blogsite is a closed page, they have likely already chosen a platform where the grievance will most definitely be seen by or shared with way too many nonbelievers. Do Christian Facebook users actually believe their posts will only be seen by believing eyes?

What would Twitter and Facebook look like if Christians resolved never again to criticize another follower of Christ in such a public fashion, especially before the stages of Matthew 18 had been carefully followed?

The next time a fellow member of your church, even your pastor, shares negative information about another believer outside the context of NTN patterns, consider another approach than replying with "Amen!" or "Thank you! Someone needs to stand up for righteousness." How about privately approaching them in humility and asking for *biblical* counsel on how you can follow the steps they just modeled for you? The awkward pause should be revealing.

We will turn our attention in the next chapter to the pattern of New Testament *experience*, demonstrating the encouraging benefits of NTN confrontation I've been explaining. But let me first reinforce Paul's pattern of instruction one more time:

> So why do you condemn another believer? Why do you look down on another believer? Remember, we will all stand before the judgment seat of God. For the Scriptures say, "As surely as I live," says the Lord, "every knee will bend to me, and every tongue will declare allegiance to God." Yes, each of us will give a personal account to God. So let's stop condemning each other. Decide instead to live in such a way that you will not cause another believer to stumble and fall. (Romans 14:10-13 NLT)

# GET THE MESSAGE?

The New Testament makes no effort to portray the early church as a group of believers who always got along, nor does it even hint that believers should ever expect to completely avoid conflict with one another.

Christ's clarion call for resolving offenses among believers in Matthew chapter 18 serves as the foundation for repeated New Testament themes about reconciliation in stages, inside the church.

With every escalating step in the Matthew 18 process of reconciliation, the intent begins and ends with the gracious expectation that the offending party will be embraced as a fully forgiven member of the family.

Instead of adhering to the stages approach, today's believers too often employ a form of confrontation completely lacking in biblical support when they speak ill of one another with nonbelievers watching.

# 4

# DARK DAYS, BRIGHT ENDINGS

If you have always felt inside that it wasn't quite right to go public with flippant and routine calling out of other Christ-followers … your gut isn't just your gut. I believe it was instead the Holy Spirit confirming in your heart what the Word of God has made abundantly clear: a pattern of instruction supported and reinforced with an encouraging pattern of experience.

Christians disagree. Christians offend. Christians sin against God, one another, and the world. While love indeed covers a multitude of sins, there are many times in our lives when the kindest thing another believer can do is to confront us in love and draw attention to the offense we have caused.

(On purpose, this book does not attempt to address the regrettable tendency in many believers to avoid confrontation altogether. This should not in any way be interpreted to mean that Christian confrontation is not needed. Many excellent writings and offerings point out the critical need for believers to practice Ephesians 4:15 by "speaking the truth in love" to one another.)

### Trouble in "Paradise"?

It is no accident that the New Testament recounts so many examples of disagreement and offense among believers. You might even say it was NTN for believers to say and do things that caused other believers distress and hurt. It really helps us today to understand this. Christians of all centuries might as well admit, "If you worship with us, you are going to get hurt." Not because it's our goal, but because it's reality. In this world, we will have tribulation (John 16:33), and, sadly, part of that tribulation comes at the hands of other believers—a result of our own sinful, stupid, selfish choices.

> **Christians of all centuries might as well admit, "If you worship with us, you are going to get hurt."**

In my role as a state denominational leader, I see this from a challenging perspective. On too many occasions, I have had the uncomfortable charge of standing beside a pastor for a very awkward and painful gathering of the congregation. Without contradicting the intent of Matthew 18, the apostle Paul prescribed this scenario. Certain situations call for rebuking spiritual elders in front of others, without showing partiality simply because they hold an esteemed position (1 Tim. 5:17-21). Congregants seldom expect to hear that their pastor committed a serious moral failure. Even though they know human nature, and they know the Scripture, they just hoped or assumed their church and their pastor were special. Now, the tears and looks of disappointment on the faces of unsuspecting saints are hard to forget.

Thankfully, most men and women in ministry leadership do live lives that, on the whole, inspire others. But when yours is the church that has to wade through the heartbreak and turmoil of a pastor resigning under duress, you understand pain and hurt in a unique way. Your heart breaks for your pastor, spouse, and family. If another person was involved in the sin, you hurt for them and their family. You weep for new believers whose fragile faith is rocked, sometimes to the point of walking away from the faith.

Then, sometimes months later, after you've finished trying to help others on their road to healing, you are hit afresh with your own grief. You sob uncontrollably. You may even get a little scared because, until now, you never knew you were capable of such deep anger.

This is just one example of why this chapter's exercise is so vital. When friction and offense erupt inside a church, there *is* a path forward. In fact, there is even reason to rejoice, in a "trying of your faith" kind of way. In His genius, God has crafted a mechanism of Christian confrontation that not only gives direction for handling the immediate challenge but also can propel the church forward with vigor.

Five varied examples from the book of Acts give us cause for hope in the midst of pain:

### Holy Fear (Acts 5:1-14)

In one of the most severe cases recorded in the New Testament, Peter confronts a husband and wife in the young and growing Jerusalem church. His name is Ananias and her name is Sapphira. (Two other men in Acts were named Ananias, but this is the first one mentioned, and his example was not one of integrity. No wonder the name never seems to make the *Top 50 Baby Boy Names* list.)

A spirit of generosity was sweeping the church, and amazingly, people's daily needs were all being met. Christians didn't *have* to sell their property or possessions, but many of them did. There was no edict that the proceeds from such transactions, in whole or in part, had to go to the church, but many people brought them anyway. Neither do we see any inference that believers had to declare the percentage of the profit being donated.

For some reason, Ananias and Sapphira decided to do all three, or to at least look like they were. Selling their property and making a sizable donation were both exemplary gestures. But they chose to go further. Likely motivated by pride, Ananias announced to the apostles that they had sold their acreage for, let's say, $50,000 and were donating it all to the church. Actually, they had sold their plot for $100,000 while electing to secretly keep fifty Gs for themselves.

Peter, the recognized authority figure of the newly formed church, confronted Ananias and Sapphira in a manner consistent with Matthew 18. He reminded Ananias that no one said they had to sell their land and, if they did sell it, it was up to them to decide how much of the proceeds, if any, would be donated to the Lord's work. So, since they were never under constraint to donate 100 percent of the profits, why did they allow Satan to influence their motives and actions? They perverted what could have otherwise been an exemplary act.

Peter sadly explained that they had lied not only to their fellow believers but also to the Holy Spirit. Through the spiritual gift of discernment or a word of knowledge, or both, the Holy Spirit revealed to Peter what Ananias and Sapphira had actually done.

What happened next was unique, mystical, and tragic all at the same time. As soon as Ananias heard Peter's challenge, he collapsed on the floor—dead! A few hours later, not having heard what happened to her husband, Sapphira received a similar challenge from Peter. Peter specifically warned her that she was about to meet the same fate as her husband. With that, she too expired on the spot.

Now there is no indication that Peter wanted them dead, or that he was given the power to strike them dead. He was simply in tune with the Holy Spirit, who gave him insight into what had happened in the dark and what was about to happen next.

Why such an extreme response by God? Theologians suggest that, for starters, it is never a small thing to lie to the Holy Spirit. Further, this wasn't just any church. At this early stage of history, this was The Church's epicenter. With stakes so high, there was no room then (nor is there today) for lying to the Holy Spirit and fostering a culture of dishonesty, greed, and pride. The upstart church could have come crashing down in its infancy if there wasn't a deep respect among its members for walking circumspectly.

In addition, church members grew in their respect for spiritually sensitive leaders such as Peter. As Acts 5:11 states, "Great fear came on the entire church and on all those who heard these things."

Despite the drama, Peter was just following protocol, confronting the couple who just lied to him and the apostles. Only those who witnessed the lie witnessed the confrontation. This we know with relative confidence.

Scripture is not specific on where this encounter happened. Could it have even taken place in someone's home where the apostles were convening? If so, then all of the confrontation seems likely to have happened in the context of believers.

But what if the confrontation happened, as is most often assumed, in a place as busy as the Jerusalem temple? Nonbelievers could not enter the temple's inner areas, but the outer courts had spots where Gentiles were permitted, as the name "Court of the Gentiles" directly implies.

The immediate context of this chapter, however, seems to imply a private confrontation, even though nonbelieving Gentiles could have been not too far away. Four clues lead to this conclusion:

1. Solomon's Porch had become the place where Christ-followers gathered. Both Acts 3:11 and Acts 5:12 say the believers, scores of them, now regularly occupied Solomon's Porch. Jesus previously taught from this location (John 10:23), and no doubt the believers felt strong association with this gathering spot. If the false offering and confrontation of Ananias and Sapphira happened there, the observation that the believers were "all with one accord in Solomon's Porch" (Acts 5:12 NKJV) paints an image of the Christ-followers at least having their own temple area in which they routinely convened and worshiped. The presence of persons with contrary views or faiths does not fit this picture.

2. Wherever they were, there was a physical entrance into and out of the room. Peter told Sapphira the young men who had buried her husband were "at the door." They

then "entered" the space where the apostles were to remove her corpse as well.

3. Sapphira was unaware that Ananias had died. Had Ananias succumbed in a crowded public venue with nonbelievers watching, or had the young men immediately announced who it was they were burying, it's impossible to imagine Sapphira walking into Peter's presence hours later with no knowledge of her husband's fate. By comparison, a lame man's healing, also near the temple, was quickly known throughout the whole town. The Jewish leaders said so (Acts 4:16). The news of Ananias's demise and burial was apparently not circulated yet, even though it would eventually spread far and wide. After Sapphira's passing, Scripture indicates the word even traveled outside the church.

4. The most obvious: No mention made of Gentiles or nonbelievers. While Acts doesn't spell out that nonbelievers were forbidden from observing these proceedings, neither is there any mention of them being present. In dozens of other encounters throughout the book of Acts, the author (Luke) is fairly detailed in listing the identities of audience members. Gentiles, as well as Jewish antagonizers whenever present, whether individuals or a whole crowd, were routinely noted. Chapter 7 in the pages ahead cites many examples of Luke's habit of identifying nonbelievers in the audience. This doesn't happen here. The tainted gift, the confrontation, and the judgment of God all seem to happen in the immediate presence of the apostles, literally, "at their feet."

In summary, there is no testimony whatsoever, or even a direct hint, that Peter's quick rebuke of either Ananias or Sapphira happened in the presence of nonbelievers. For that matter, neither is there reason to believe it happened in front of any believers who were not present to observe the lie Ananias had told, even though word of both deaths clearly spread thereafter.

Granted, it's a bit challenging to continue the Matthew 18 steps of confrontation with someone God has already stricken dead! But Peter at least handled the first step appropriately, in alignment with Christ's guidance. To do otherwise would have been out of context with all other confrontations in Acts and throughout the New Testament.

Pay attention to the fact that the news spreading was not simply about how two Christians had messed up. It included the power of a holy and righteous God. If it had been only about two greedy liars ("there goes those hypocritical Christians"), the public's response would have been ridicule instead of fear. The church would have likely declined, as it has in multiple places recently; instead, it mushroomed! The very next paragraph reports that "believers were increasingly added to the Lord, crowds of both men and women" (v. 14). Many scholars believe the events of Acts 1—5 all happened within a year or so. Peter's obedient following of NTN protocol fostered an environment that God deemed holy, and the church grew in spite of this case of pride and deceit in the ranks.

When the Holy Spirit senses the hearts of church leaders in alignment with the Word, the headline outside the church can become *How God is Moving* instead of *How Christians are Failing.* Isn't this what our hearts all long for today?

## Pure Religion (Acts 6:1-7)

Instead of involving just one or two people, the offense in this next case was a group situation. Hellenistic (Greek-oriented) widows in the church were not receiving the same care and consideration as the church's Hebrew widows, especially at mealtimes. Rumblings and frustrations began to bubble up. So church leaders called all the disciples together. Confrontation happened inside the church, with the appropriate parties. There is no testimony here in Acts that disgruntled Christians were gossiping to their unbelieving friends about inept church leadership. And this even had ethnic overtones. Hellenistic members could have been offended and gone off to start their own congregation, giving the church a sour reputation in the community. Thankfully, that didn't happen.

Because protocol was followed, the complaint was aired and deemed to be legitimate. The remedy came swiftly, with the appointment of qualified church leaders who could address the widows' needs. Those appointed were likely received well by the frustrated Hellenists; they were vetted ("full of the Holy Spirit and of wisdom") and all seven men had Greek names. The widows were taken care of, the apostles were freed up to pray and preach the Word instead of working in the kitchen, and additional leaders were raised up and used in their gifts—it became a multiple-win situation.

And guess what. Verse 7 reports, "So the word of God spread, and the number of the disciples grew rapidly in Jerusalem." Many people actually got saved as a result of this confrontation. And no one died this time! The exclamation mark comes with the additional notation "... and a great number of the priests were obedient to the faith." Booyah!

## Three's Company? (Acts 15:36-41)

We all know what it's like to hear something that raises our eyebrows, at least a little. Maybe the way a husband uncomfortably shrugged when his wife asked him about an acquaintance. Or, how when we asked a co-worker why they seemed so quiet today, they slowly replied, "Just thinking about something." We say to ourselves, *Am I the only one who noticed that?*

But if no one else seems to question, we often conclude we must have heard it wrong or that we're making a bigger deal out of the situation than necessary. However, if the situation later blows up, we find ourselves saying, "Aha! I knew there was something there!"

Such is the case in Acts 13—14. Paul and Barnabas are leaving Antioch to undertake what we now refer to as their First Missionary Journey. A young associate named Mark (actually, John Mark) is tagging along to help.

After ministry in several towns and regions in the Mediterranean, it is noted without any commentary that Mark suddenly decides to go back to Jerusalem by himself (Acts 13:13). That's it. He leaves. No comment. Paul and Barnabas continue on. Entire towns hear the gospel. Miracles happen. No harm, no foul, apparently.

Until chapter 15. Having completed the journey by celebrating all the news of conversions and church plants with leaders in both Antioch and Jerusalem, Paul and Barnabas are prayed up and ready to head out from Antioch for Mission #2. Until Barnabas drops the "Oh, by the way" bombshell. "Paul, I've been thinking. Wouldn't it be great if Mark went along on this trip, too?"

Um, in a word—*No!* Paul is having none of it. And now we understand that it had really been kind of a big deal when Mark bailed on the first excursion. Barnabas sees potential in Mark, despite his disappointing debut. But Paul won't budge. In fact, the only way they can resolve this conflict is to part ways and go on separate missionary journeys. Barnabas takes Mark to Cyprus, while Paul buddies up with Silas and heads to Syria and Cilicia.

What a great illustration of staying inside the boundaries of NTN in the midst of sharp disagreement. We cannot unequivocally conclude that Barnabas was wrong for wanting to give Mark another chance. Neither can we be absolutely sure that Paul was wrong because he didn't think it wise. Two great Christian leaders had a heated debate and concluded the best solution under the circumstances was to amend their previous plans and part ways. It happens. It happens a lot.

Was Barnabas right? From what we know, possibly! All Christians, especially Paul, know how essential it is to the gospel that we need second chances ... or even a third. Barnabas could have been downright shocked and angry that Paul, of all people, was refusing to show some flexibility when it was Paul himself who had been the recipient of Barnabas's good will and mentoring in Paul's early days as a believer (see Acts 9:26-28 and 11:22-26). Plus, Barnabas knew they were heading first to Cyprus. The island of Cyprus had been their initial stop on the first journey, and they had already decided to revisit the same places in order to strengthen all those new churches. Acts 4:36 reveals Cyprus was Barnabas's home, and Colossians 4:10 indicates Mark may have been related to Barnabas. So, when the rift happened, is it a surprise that Barnabas went to his home territory as planned, and took a relative with him, while Paul and a new teammate, Silas, headed northwest instead? Is it reasonable that family plans sometimes influence ministry decisions?

On the other hand, was Paul right? From what we read, possibly! Traveling in those days, although greatly improved thanks to Roman engineering, was still life-threatening and exhausting. Add to that the job hazards of preaching Christianity. On that very upcoming journey, Paul and Silas were severely beaten and imprisoned in Philippi. For Mark's own sake, maybe it was simply too soon for him to play an integral role on such a harrowing expedition. Further, Scripture notes that the church leaders prayed and commissioned Paul and Silas before they left (Acts 15:40). There is no such statement of approval about Barnabas taking Mark to Cyprus.

We simply don't know for sure. Unfortunately, we don't read of any more direct interaction between Paul and Barnabas after that conflict. Maybe their paths crossed again, one or the other of them apologized, and they were good buddies. Maybe both scratched their heads the rest of their lives, somewhat convinced the other party really missed the boat on that one.

> **We see no evidence that Paul and Barnabas hated each other, complained about one another, or shared their frustrations with nonbelievers.**

Thankfully, we read that Paul defended Barnabas years after their disagreement (1 Cor. 9:6). He also expressed a high regard for Mark, affirming his worth and their mutual interaction in the work of the ministry (Col. 4:10, Philem. 24, 2 Tim. 4:11). Many scholars believe this is the Mark who wrote the Gospel by the same name.

Heated disagreements between Christians happen—even between Christians who deeply love and respect one another, as Paul and Barnabas did. This story gives us assurance that seeing eye-to-eye on every matter is not instantaneous, or even inevitable.

If this conflict had been about sin, then either Paul or Barnabas should have repented as soon as possible. But this was a judgment call confrontation. NTN measures for conflict resolution still guide us. We see no evidence that Paul and Barnabas hated each other, complained about one another, or shared their frustrations with nonbelievers.

And as a result of Paul refusing to violate protocol, people got saved again!—many people in a variety of towns and provinces. Churches were launched. If Paul had gone straight to Cyprus with Barnabas and Mark, we may have never heard about the churches in Philippi, Corinth, or Ephesus (or be reading Philippians, Ephesians, or 1 and 2 Corinthians today).

## The Apollos Mission (Acts 18:24-26)

All over the globe, people are being saved, baptized, and discipled. Almost without exception, other Christians are involved. But God always deserves the glory because His Spirit, not ours, draws them in; Christ's sacrifice, not ours, provides for their atonement.

Paul described his time in the city of Corinth this way: "I have planted, Apollos watered, but God gave the increase" (1 Cor. 3:6). Boy, did he ever plant! It should catch our attention, however, that of all the people he could have named as he continued his word picture, he chose Apollos.

Apparently, some in the Corinthian church were foolishly starting to choose sides. Instead of being content (and obedient) to identify themselves simply as disciples of Christ, some were choosing to self-identify as followers of Paul, while others preferred to align with Apollos, while others were loyal to Peter. Paul famously made his point that no single Bible teacher, no matter how effective or well-known, causes spiritual growth; only God can do that.

But this controversy certainly testifies to what an influential teacher and apologist Apollos had become over the years. It also reminds us of the NTN manner in which Apollos, as a younger preacher, had been confronted by two wise and caring mentors, Priscilla and her husband, Aquila. According to Acts 18:24-26, they heard Apollos preaching about the water baptism practiced by John (which Jesus underwent Himself). It became clear to them that, although Apollos was very aware of the Scriptures, something was missing.

He had apparently not yet heard about the baptism of the Holy Spirit, which first took place on Pentecost in Jerusalem and was now becoming commonplace among believers as the gospel continued to spread. Jews were being baptized in the Spirit, speaking in tongues, and being used in the gifts of the Spirit. So were Gentiles such as Cornelius and all his household (Acts 10). In the verses that follow this Acts 18 account, Paul discovers more believers in Ephesus who resembled Apollos. They said they had heard about John's water baptism but not about Spirit baptism. Paul shared about Pentecost and prayed with them, and they began speaking in tongues immediately.

There has certainly been robust debate in evangelical circles regarding the baptism of the Holy Spirit and the accompanying manifestation of speaking in tongues. However, all viewpoints can appreciate the gentle manner in which Priscilla and Aquila confronted Apollos. Instead of immediately rebuking him in front of other believers there in the synagogue, "they took him aside and explained to him the way of God more accurately" (Acts 18:26 NKJV). Another version describes an even more intimate setting: "They invited him to their home" (NIV). Rather than exposing outsiders to firsthand evidence of disagreement, they kept the matter inside a small circle.

Had Apollos actually sinned against Priscilla and Aquila? No, which is why Matthew 18 correction might not seem to apply line-for-line. Nonetheless, the spirit of that type of confrontation serves as a healthy starting point for most disagreements between believers. The numerous passages and examples cited in the previous chapter and this one substantiate the stages approach as the Christian's "gold standard" for resolving differences.

And here's why. Apollos not only survived that moment of private correction, he blossomed and thrived as a preacher—so much, in fact, that Paul had to later remind the Corinthians that neither he nor Apollos deserved any glory. Any growth in our own lives or in the kingdom is a direct result of God's influence and power.

*The New York Times* ran an article in 2014 on world-renowned Hillsong Church that examined its stance on homosexuality.[23] Multiple news outlets and news anchors with household names have interviewed Pastor Brian Houston of Hillsong Australia and Pastor Carl Lentz of Hillsong NYC about this subject. Many liberals, of course, are skeptical of any church with an evangelical label, especially one that is apparently in the Pentecostal camp. A number of conservatives are concerned about Hillsong as well, due to a perceived lack of clarity on biblical sexuality coming from the church's pastors. Both groups seem put off that so many people are finding Hillsong's version of faith so attractive. Hillsong's pastors say they are wholehearted believers in the Bible, and they are simply and intentionally steering clear of pigeonholing labels that prove counterproductive to people finding Christ.

The *Times* piece didn't have to look far to find a critique coming from the Religious Right. "Let's be clear that this is not the route of faithfulness," declared a blogger on a prominent website. "When I read stuff like this, my reaction isn't anger. It's an eye-roll. Churches should know better than to believe the myth that accommodation will swell their ranks. The opposite happens."[24] The headline of the blog? "A Church in Exile."

Imagine if Priscilla and Aquila were around today. Pretend that they lived near New York City or Sydney, Australia. And assume, for this hypothetical, that they would have concerns about Hillsong's approach on the issue of homosexuality.

Can you picture them crafting an "Open Letter" criticizing Hillsong's leadership? Would you see them on primetime cable news programs explaining to believers and unbelievers alike why Pastor Houston or Pastor Lentz are leading people astray? I can't envision them even troubling the apostle Paul about this.

Instead, following Matthew 18, we would see them inviting Houston or Lentz into a private place for coffee and some genuine discussion about Scripture. Doesn't that sound an awful lot like the Golden Rule? And even if their efforts produced no immediate response, you simply wouldn't see them joining any effort that would give nonbelievers a front row seat for disagreements between believers.

### "Faithful are the Wounds of a Friend" (Acts 15 and Galatians 2)

Apparently, Paul and Barnabas had had their disagreements before. According to Paul's version in Galatians 2:11-21, his major beef was with Peter. But perhaps the most serious, albeit subtle, charge was leveled at his close friend and fellow evangelist: "... even Barnabas was carried away by their hypocrisy" (v. 13). The comment reads like it was one thing for Peter to cave under pressure, but Barnabas? Paul's mentor. Mature leader. Encouraging Barnabas. Yes, *even* Barnabas had disappointed Paul.

Ouch!

This is an interesting case of group confrontation. Although Bible scholars are not certain about the timing of the two meetings described in Galatians 2 and Acts 15, the principle of Matthew 18 confrontation remains intact. To set the stage: According to Acts 14, after Paul and Barnabas returned to the Antioch church at the conclusion of their first missionary trip, they gave a celebratory report and praised the Lord for all the gospel advancements that had taken place. The celebration evaporated into dissension, however, in the first verse of chapter 15. Jewish believers (called *Judaizers*) later came to Antioch teaching that Gentile men could not really, truly be saved unless they became circumcised ... yes, even if they were grown men.

Ouch, again!

Paul and Barnabas sharply disagreed with them, and were then sent to Jerusalem to seek the opinion of the apostles and church elders on this divisive issue. Acts 15 records that the church leaders there wrestled with the matter. Peter took to the floor to argue strongly that salvation was by the grace of the Lord Jesus alone. In the end, Paul and Barnabas were sent back to Antioch with additional church representatives to deliver a written statement from church elders, stating that they had given no blessing to the men who were pressuring Gentiles to be circumcised. Circumcision could not possibly be an added requirement of salvation.

Whether or not that was the same meeting outlined in the opening verses of Galatians 2, Paul's frustration in this chapter is understandable. Peter knew better than most that there was no difference between Jew and Gentile in God's eyes. He had, after all, received a vision about this very issue (see Acts 10). God's plan was for both Jews and Gentiles to worship Him. Due to Peter's hesitance, he got to see the vision no less than three times. Shortly thereafter, the vision became reality as Peter witnessed the Holy Spirit being poured out on the Gentile household of Cornelius. They all spoke in tongues just like Jewish believers did. If Galatians 2 and Acts 15 *do* reference the same event, Paul had even more reason to be irate!

Regardless of the timing, this we know. In Galatians 2:11, Paul explains that Peter himself came down to Antioch. He apparently gave further support to the church's affirmation that salvation was by grace alone. Peter had already joined Paul and Barnabas in robust fellowship with the Gentile believers in Antioch. Jews and Gentiles, circumcised and uncircumcised, ate and interacted with one another, unified by their mutual faith in Christ. In the view of many scholars, Peter was now practicing what he himself preached when he previously defended the Gentile believers at the Jerusalem council (Acts 15). Yes, salvation is indeed through the grace of our Lord Jesus ... unless, apparently, some strong-willed Jewish Christians show up.

And they did. These were the kind who still held firmly to the circumcision requirement and were vocal about it. The peer pressure they inflicted was apparently too much for Peter and the other Jewish Christians to handle, *even* Barnabas. To Paul's shock and dismay, they actually quit eating with the uncircumcised Gentile Christians in Antioch. They withdrew fellowship from them and separated themselves, all because they feared the reaction of the circumcision bullies.

Paul confronted Peter's hypocritical behavior in front of the whole group, because they were all guilty. He followed Christ's confrontation protocol by going directly to the person(s) causing the offense, and not raising the concern in front of nonbelievers. That this form of hypocrisy with ethnic overtones was properly addressed, and that it happened sooner rather than later, fostered the continuing salvation of Gentiles during those early years of the church. Can you imagine the incredible difficulty of reaching Gentiles with the gospel, then or now, had this matter not been successfully handled?

We don't read in Galatians 2 of Peter's response to Paul's rebuke. But there is no indication that he resisted Paul or lost favor among the Gentiles. To the contrary, Peter's own epistles authored years later were written mainly to Gentile converts. There, Peter affirms the teaching about salvation they had already received from ... who else? Paul! Peter further notes that Paul has been given wisdom and is able to communicate things that a lot of other people find hard to grasp (2 Peter 3:15-16).

## More Evidence

This account and the others cited previously in this chapter display a powerful pattern of experience throughout Acts backing up a striking pattern of instruction throughout the New Testament. Christian confrontation is meant to happen *in stages, inside the church.*

Of course, there are even more examples in the New Testament church where believers caused other believers pain and confusion. Some include:

- John warned the church about a troublemaker named Diotrephes and testified that he had sent letters and messengers to Diotrephes already, which Diotrephes ignored or rejected. John said that he might visit the church in the future and would confront Diotrephes in person at that time. (3 John 9-10)
- Paul makes an oblique reference to an offending brother who had repented after being confronted. Paul encouraged that he should now be robustly loved and affirmed. [Some scholars speculate this might have been the incestuous brother previously referenced in 1 Corinthians 5 who had to be handed over to Satan for a season.] (2 Corinthians 2:5-11)
- Paul assigned Timothy the task of correcting false teachers in the Ephesian church who were placing a distorted emphasis on Old Testament law and genealogies. (1 Timothy 1:3-7)

- Paul warned Timothy about Hymenaeus and Alexander, "whom I have delivered to Satan that they may learn not to blaspheme." (1 Timothy 1:20)
- Paul gave Timothy yet another directive: "Do not receive an accusation against an elder, except before two or three witnesses. Rebuke in the presence of everyone those who sin, that the rest also may fear." (1 Timothy 5:19-20)
- Paul lamented that "all those who are in Asia have turned away from me, including Phygelus and Hermogenes." Timothy needed to know about this. Such a statement tells us that when people abandon you or the church, there may be little you can do to further confront or reconcile them. But you can warn other Christians. This is often played out today in communities where pastors have forged good relationships with one another. They can warn fellow ministers to be on the lookout for certain players in the kingdom who leave without providing opportunity for working out differences. (2 Timothy 1:15)
- Paul warned Timothy to "avoid profane foolish babblings, for they will increase to more ungodliness, and their word will spread like gangrene: Among them are Hymenaeus and Philetus, who have erred concerning the truth, saying that the resurrection has already occurred, and who overthrow the faith of some." Paul had already mentioned Hymenaeus and his confrontation in 1 Timothy 1:20. These were divisive and dangerous heretics, the kind Paul referenced in Titus 3:10. He thought they might deserve one or two

confrontation sessions before being excommunicated. (2 Timothy 2:16-18)

- Paul told Titus to rebuke the Cretans sharply so they could become sound in their faith. (Titus 1:13)

In these and other cases throughout the New Testament we are again reminded of helpful truths:

1. Confrontation among believers is to be expected.
2. Direct and discreet confrontation is to be employed before widening the circle.
3. Sometimes the offending party does an about-face; sometimes not.
4. Rebuke and correction of believers is not intended for nonbelievers to view.
5. Conscientious Christian confrontation creates an atmosphere where the church thrives.

## Cover Up Instead?

In an age with a seemingly growing appetite for unfiltered transparency, some might rightly wonder if we should work so hard to hide our dirty laundry. "Doesn't this just add to the complaint that so many Christians are fake? Isn't it hypocritical to make the world think we get along when, many times, we don't?"

Let me put it this way: Are you lacking authenticity when you fail to tell your neighbors that you had a heated argument with your in-laws? Is it being hypocritical when you preserve your child's dignity by keeping secret her recent run-in with the principal? Fake and hypocritical labels apply, correctly, when we say or even insinuate we have no moral weak spots. But broadcasting that we never have any disagreements is altogether different from skillfully working out our differences behind closed doors.

While it's true that New Testament believers kept their many disagreements from the view of nonbelievers, they clearly didn't hide *everything* from them. In the chapters to come, we will smile over and over as we explore the powerful encounters believers regularly had with nonbelievers.

# GET THE
# MESSAGE?

When New Testament believers handled offenses and disagreements without violating the principles of Matthew 18, the immediate challenge was navigated while consistently propelling the church forward with vigor.

Dealing with conflict in stages, inside the church, creates an atmosphere where God's Spirit can cause the church to grow, even in the aftermath of misbehaving Christians (Ananias and Sapphira).

Even when Christians sharply disagree, God blesses our ministry and causes His church to attract new believers when we refuse to let bitterness grow or speak ill of each other (Paul, Barnabas and Mark).

Christian leaders can powerfully model initiating and receiving healthy criticism when we address concerns with each other in private, in stages (Priscilla, Aquila, and Apollos).

Over and over again, the New Testament provides healthy examples of Christian leaders directly challenging sinning saints inside the church while routinely and skillfully avoiding the involvement of nonbelievers in the process.

# 5

## GIVE 'EM SOMETHING TO TALK ABOUT

For the reasons previously outlined, confrontation among believers needs to stay inside the church. But God doesn't want us hiding ourselves from the world. No, truth be told, He's kind of a show-off. With the stakes so high for the eternities of humanity, His genius in this regard is, in a word, *epic*.

Few moments in life cause a deeper sense of satisfaction to parents than when their children genuinely seem to like each other. From the exhausted mother who is simply grateful that the two kicking and screaming toddlers eventually opt to get along (at least long enough for a short nap) to the deep sigh of the dying father as he smiles at the sight of his grown children forgiving and embracing the black sheep who finally came home, most moms and dads find tremendous peace when their kids love and care for another. No doubt that instinct comes from the character of our heavenly Father, whose DNA rests inside each one of us.

But in the eternal enterprise that is the family of God, caring for one another is more than just warm fuzzies; it's life or death. Jesus Himself instructed us to love one another because it has such a direct and forever impact on those who are not yet part of His family. "By *this* all men will know that you are my disciples …" (John 13:35). And what is "this"? "… if you have love for one another."

When we love another believer like Jesus loved us, the immediate audience is of course that particular Christian (or Christians). Meanwhile, the larger audience who sees the moment or the aftermath of how exceptionally we treat one another must be kept in constant consideration. As intentional as is the repeated directive to avoid opposing fellow believers in front of the world, the opposite is true when it comes to nonbelievers witnessing the love and care we show one another. The latter must be carried out routinely with the awareness that God wants His children's love for one another on full display. It's our secret weapon and part of His master plan!

## Not Just a "Suggestion"

There is a clear pattern of New Testament instruction and an abundance of New Testament experience on this concept. In fact, few commandments are stated more often, by more writers, in more ways across the New Testament than to show to other Christians the kind of love that Christ has shown to us.

And it is nothing short of an outright *commandment,* no matter how we slice it. As adamant as the guidelines are for confronting and critiquing in private, so are the commands for loving and caring in public.

For starters, to remove any confusion, Jesus actually called it a "new commandment," something He did for no other teaching: "A new commandment I give to you, that you love one another" (John 13:34). Later that same evening, He said it again: "This is My commandment: that you love one another" (John 15:12). In another passage, (Matt. 22:37-40), Jesus catapulted this directive to stratospheric levels of importance by declaring it was second only to the greatest commandment, to love the Lord our God. Those two commandments combined, He added, were the foundation for the entirety of the law and the prophets.

This pattern of instruction continues in the New Testament, well beyond the words of Christ in the Gospels. Like Jesus, the apostle Paul commands love to everyone, believer and nonbeliever. And, like Jesus, he explains that we should show a priority toward believers, doing good to everyone, "especially to those who are of the household of faith" (Gal. 6:10). John likewise repeats the direct instruction of Jesus that believers should love another (1 John 4:7).

With Paul's masterpiece in 1 Corinthians 13, commonly called the Love Chapter, or with John's frequent referral to believers as the "Beloved," we can overlook the fact that Peter also wrote quite prolifically about love. Yes, that brash fisherman, Peter. Do you automatically credit him when you hear these admonitions to love fellow Christians?

- Love one another deeply with a pure heart. (1 Peter 1:22)
- Love the brotherhood. (1 Peter 2:17)
- Above all things, have unfailing love for one another, because love covers a multitude of sins. (1 Peter 4:8)
- Greet one another with a kiss of love. (1 Peter 5:14)
- To your brotherly kindness, [add] love. (2 Peter 1:7)

Based on the sheer volume of admonitions to show extraordinary love for brothers and sisters in Christ, who could conclude that we should do otherwise?

But it's not just the *words* of Jesus and the apostles. It never is! The pattern of experience comes along and bolsters this pattern of instruction. Over and over again, the New Testament showcases believers actively demonstrating love to one another through a variety of tangible and meaningful means. They prayed for one another often. They opened their homes and provided warm hospitality. They sent offerings in times of need. At great risk and personal sacrifice, many of them traveled together in ministry. And, they unquestionably spent a lot of time in fellowship and discipleship with one another, verbalizing their mutual love and support as well.

## Not Always Easy

It is worth noting that the challenging physical, financial, and social circumstances under which the early Christians offered incredible love and care were often, frankly, beyond the comprehension of many Western believers. Despite threats to their freedom as citizens, their societal status, and their very lives, those first believers demonstrated to their contemporaries and to all of us the sacrificial commitment required to fully live out the commandment to love one another.

That's not to say their sacrifice negated their joy. Walking out their faith in Christ actually had the opposite effect. Loving one another in seasons of great challenge produced immeasurable joy and satisfaction. In the final verses of Acts 2, thousands of new believers in Christ shared tremendous gladness in the process of meeting each other's needs and worshiping in unity, for all the world to see. Acts 4:34 and following testifies to the reality that believers who care for one another facilitate God's divine supply for the basic necessities of life. The next chapter offers further testimony (5:12) that the believers enjoyed unity. Acts 6 recounts the believers' efforts to show loving care to the church's widows, the "pure religion" we just talked about, courtesy of James's instruction.

We need to hear this. With the cacophony of voices, even Christian voices, clamoring for attention and action, it is entirely within our ability to bring a smile to God's face. Even before the sun goes down today! We'll never fully grasp how much joy our heavenly Father derives from watching His family love one another.

> **With the cacophony of voices clamoring for attention, it is entirely within our ability to bring a smile to God's face.**

In the first few chapters of Acts, so soon after Christ had departed, how pleased God must have been to see His children demonstrating selfless, Christlike love to one another, especially to those in the church who were the most vulnerable. While they still had significant lessons to learn about loving one another completely, you can just hear all of heaven shouting, "They're starting to get it! They really are!"

This pattern of experience continues throughout the New Testament. We read more than once about generous offerings for fellow believers. Often under threat of persecution, believers came to each other's aid in times of peril. They frequently told each other of their love. As we have already examined, the thoughtful manner in which they corrected and admonished one another is another solid example of love. Christians loved other Christians deeply, sincerely, and sacrificially. While it is also true that Christians showed incredible love and good will to all people, even hostile nonbelievers, they were especially kind toward one another, in harmony with the instructions of Jesus and the apostles.

## Taking Stock Today

So what's going on now? We'll get to our audience of nonbelievers momentarily. But even inside the church: Can we believers say with confidence that Christ's body is uniformly avoiding the public ridicule of fellow believers while loving each other as Christ loved us?

Preachers have long warned us that believers can become deceived. The Devil, we are reminded, has no authority over the child of God. Could this be one of those areas where, without any power over us at all, our Enemy keeps scoring victories when he flashes something sparkly to take our eye off the target? In a culture where genuine, sacrificial love by all believers for one another would shine in bright contrast between God's people and the world, and make Jesus look really good, we too often willingly lay down our weapons. We forget that loving fellow believers is our ace in the hole! LeBron James is right there, so to speak, ready to lead our team ... but all we do is pat him on the back occasionally. We look his way and nod every once in a while, leaving him on the bench as the score is going the wrong direction. Who does that!

It has become so commonplace we don't notice it anymore. In family gatherings, we speak ill of Uncle Bill, a believer, behind his back—but in front of cousins who don't know Christ. That, of course, is on top of the fact that we've never bothered to talk to Uncle Bill about whatever shortcoming we think he has. At the office or in social gatherings where nonbelievers are present, we join in gossiping about a prominent believer who may have made a mistake. On social media, we call out other believers for their sins or chastise them for their resistance to see things the way we do, in full view of the unsaved.

In too many ways, especially for believers and church leaders who know the counsel of God's Word, we are falling prey to the Devil's pitiful but effective attempts to distract us and negate our witness. Our siblings and cousins and in-laws should not see us dishing out the same treatment of family that they see in other settings. They should instead leave our Thanksgiving and birthday celebrations and Super Bowl parties shaking their heads at what they just heard. "Wow, they've got something I don't have, and I want it. Bad!"

The political, generational, racial, and social divides that seem to bombard everyone daily should not only stand in stark contrast to what nonbelievers see in Christians, they should serve as the perfect arenas to propel the name of Jesus front and center as the amazing answer that He is. Twenty-first century challenges did not escape our Creator's foresight in crafting the perfect approach for His children to live out the gospel. It's holy clickbait! When the world sees young people praying for one another as they did in the spontaneous 2016 West Virginia high school revival, it grabs eyes and hearts nowadays, and holds on. TV newscasters, among others, couldn't resist spreading that compelling story.[25] When black and white Christ-followers worship and pray together, genuinely loving one another without pushing political agendas, the world takes notice and collectively drools.

Let's use these stories to promote Jesus, first and foremost, and then watch the good that happens to all of us as believers, and the by-product of community healing that comes when we make uplifting Christ our goal.

This is not a magic wand to wave away all challenges inside the church, which are real. But it is by far the most pragmatic and effective approach we can take for the main issue of saving the world, and all the sub-issues that plague humanity.

### More than an App

Of course, it is neither easy nor automatic to show love to other believers, privately or publicly. Staples has yet to create an Easy Button for this. Apple and Android can compete all they want, but there will never be a hassle-free app for loving one another. I have discovered this powerful truth: Just because I am a Christian doesn't mean I no longer irritate or offend other Christians. In some cases, loving a believer becomes *more* of a challenge. Brothers and sisters expect better behavior out of born-again saints like me and you.

> Apple and Android can compete all they want, but there will never be a hassle-free app for loving one another.

So if God Almighty doesn't love me any more when I get saved (because He can't), that's a good clue that some of His children might struggle with loving me more, too (not because they can't, but because I can get on their nerves so badly). But we have to try, and keep trying. Letting the world know that we're Christ-followers by the way we love one another is the proverbial rising tide that lifts all ships.

Even if you and I disagree sharply on doctrine or politics, when I see you loving Jesus, it softens my heart toward your perspective. When you see me exalting the name of the Savior who means more to you than life itself, you are naturally more eager to handle me with respect and dignity. At the foot of the cross, manmade walls come crashing down. We are then free to have serious and challenging discussions, out of the world's view, but in the full view of heaven, where our absolute best chance for reconciliation lies.

So, just as we have somehow missed the impact it could have on nonbelievers for Christ-followers to handle their disputes inside the church, have we neglected the public side of that coin, too? What if news outlets and periodicals had to send reporters to cover how one group of Christians outrageously helped another? Some radio and TV preachers consistently affirm other preachers and Christian leaders, even their "competition"—but what if they all did? What if we daily saturated social media with sincere and positive comments demonstrating how much we love and appreciate God's children? At the risk of messing with Google's vaunted algorithms, it might be worth a shot! Could loving one another lavishly and publicly be part of God's intentional strategy to catch the attention of nonbelievers, too?

### New Testament Example

What happened in the book of Acts when believers took incredible care of other believers? There are many striking statements, many powerful miracles recorded, many dynamic stories of dramatic conversions. But did you notice the audacious claim of Acts 4:34, which says, "There was no one among them who lacked"? Can you imagine the impact a label like that would have in our communities if it were known that no one at our church, not one person who worships Jesus with us, lacked for any basic necessities? None! Wouldn't that kind of reputation garner curiosity, if not intense investigation?

How is that even possible? *None of them had any need.* Is this possibly a case of the author (Luke) taking a little license with the facts? Since he later recounted the severe hardships faced by the church and the apostles, it doesn't seem likely that Luke would exaggerate to get a positive spin. So, let's unpack this. A miracle like this deserves our attention.

These are, after all, the followers of Jesus who were there and participated when He fed thousands with a few fish and some loaves of bread. They knew it was normal to expect divine provision. So with Jesus now gone, maybe they fervently prayed over their food every day, and it miraculously multiplied on occasion. Perhaps they laid hands on the collection plate, and the coins spontaneously reproduced. Though that is not what we read, we shouldn't automatically rule out the possibility of the supernatural in every circumstance.

But imagine for a moment the extreme practicality of a group of people who were totally devoted to the teachings of Jesus. On the income side, Acts says more than once that believers were incredibly generous, even selling their property and possessions to contribute to the local church. Scripture does not indicate that donors began living in the streets, homeless, because they had sold all their property. Perhaps some did, or moved in with relatives because their devotion to spreading the gospel moved them to give everything they had. Quite likely, those who had any "extras" such as land or livestock or jewelry they did not need were impressed to contribute as much as they could. And they did so with great joy!

All this sounds strange to those who have never given generously and cheerfully to the Lord's work. But it is one of the most fulfilling habits believers enjoy.

Rick Warren's testimony about tithing is becoming well known in Christian circles. Long before he became a best-selling author and world-famous pastor, he and his wife agreed to tithe faithfully and give generously. In fact, when they first got married, they committed to give an additional 1 percent per year, above the 10 percent they were already tithing. Decades later, they continue to give very liberally, and God has not ceased to take care of their financial needs.

If you were skeptical about the claims of Christianity but witnessed steady doses of people being healed and delivered from demons and addictions, wouldn't you be impressed? Miraculous signs accompanying the preaching of the gospel (then and now) attract people to Jesus. The blessing and favor of the Lord combined with the generosity of enthusiastic and reproducing believers goes a long way toward explaining the phenomenon that no believers in the Jerusalem church in those early days lacked for the basics. And, that's just the income side.

But what about minimizing expenses? Did that have any role to play? While the early Jerusalem example did not take years to manifest, conversion to Christ could reduce expenses in both the short term and over the long haul. Would the ability for Christians with diseases and ailments to be healed through the NTN prayer of faith impact the amount of money they needed for medical bills? Absolutely. Would medical expenses be further reduced when the community of believers abandoned harmful habits such as addictions to food, wine, and illicit sex? All things being equal, would everyday living expenses come down when people applied Christ-honoring fiscal discipline so they weren't overspending on nonessentials? When every able-bodied person was working as hard and as honestly for their employers as they possibly could? Would the expenses of divorce or having children out of wedlock be reduced in a population of people who were waiting till marriage for sex and then remaining faithful to their spouse? Wouldn't expenses drop in a community where people refused to steal, destroy, or physically harm one another?

In churches today where the gospel is fully preached, it's common to hear the story of the man or woman whose financial disciplines become healthier when they are set free from sinful habits. Money wasted on harmful choices is now available for more generous giving to the church's efforts. People in general earn more money when they remain more employable than when their personal life and habits are spiraling out of control. This completes the cycle and bumps up income again.

Considering the real potential for dramatic generosity and healthy spending habits, with both sides of the equation experiencing the supernatural favor of God to increase income and decrease expenses, the prospect of a church full of committed believers whose basic needs were more routinely being met doesn't seem like pie in the sky at all. The nonbelievers in our community will know that we are Christ's disciples when we love one another this unreservedly!

Visual aids like this seem more doable as long as healthy NTN parameters are in place. Testimonies of God's faithfulness need to be regularly celebrated, as Paul did over and over. Teaching from Scripture on the importance of generosity must always remain front and center. Pride, dishonesty, or favoritism associated with giving must be avoided at all costs. Believers whose actions demonstrate they are not serious about growing in their faith must be rebuked and corrected in love, regardless of whether they're relatively wealthy or needy. Church leaders must be willing to show the kind of love that was NTN by disciplining and, if necessary, removing from their ranks those who claim to be Christ-followers while ignoring repeated attempts at loving correction. Nothing dampens a giving heart more than knowing that precious funds are being disbursed in an imprudent manner inconsistent with biblical guidelines. A repeated theme in Proverbs is how we shouldn't encourage or get swept up in a fool's misbehavior.

### Enlarging the Circle

At this point, we turn our focus to loving our neighbor. Even loving our enemies. The primary directives to love God and then love fellow believers in an extraordinary fashion fuel our ability to show love to the world.

Thankfully, there are examples of outrageously generous churches across the globe that routinely engage in extravagant and ongoing efforts to minister compassion to the poor and hurting in their communities. But that is not the reality for many other congregations. Too many Christian churches find themselves in the frustrating state of always having more people with needs than personnel and financial resources to do something substantial and long-lasting about it. Our experience today is not lining up with the New Testament's pattern. What gives?

"Let us do good to all people," says the verse in Galatians cited earlier. Since there will always be tremendous human need, won't any group of believers that attempts to love and do good to everyone, even their enemies, be in a perpetual state of empty cupboards? Is your church expected to do something about all the physical and financial needs across your community? God provides rain for the just and unjust alike, so doesn't He want the needs of every beating heart to be met, even if they have not yet surrendered to Him?

The friendly skies give us some insight as we consider the audience of nonbelievers watching us. The vast majority of airline passengers will never experience the emergency scenarios they are prepped for prior to takeoff. What the flight attendant recites feels counterintuitive to parents. You can quote it by heart if you fly every once in a while.

When the oxygen masks descend from the ceiling, you are told to avoid doing what would feel instinctual in that moment if your young child is seated near you. Instead of reaching over to place the mask on the helpless, possibly frantic child, resist the temptation to intervene. Help yourself first. Put the mask over your mouth and nose, and breathe normally (yeah, right!). Then, reach over and help your child.

In severe situations at such high altitudes, your child may actually go unconscious for a few moments until oxygen supply is restored. As horrible as that sounds, not breathing for a few seconds is rarely critical. It's no fun, but we can rebound nicely after access to quality air is resumed.

But if you decide to reverse the routine, devastating consequences could result. If you avoid establishing your own connection to a healthy supply and try to assist the helpless one first, you may not be successful before you both pass out, and possibly succumb. If the child is helped but the adult blacks out, the chances are heightened that the child will not be able to return the help, and injury or death could occur. Further, depending on what was going on with the plane, a breathing child could still incur injury or death without the guidance of a conscious parent.

I've heard that warning countless times and am thankful I've not had to act out on what I've (hopefully) learned. It makes complete sense to the rational person. Living it out, under stressful circumstances, would be the challenge.

Is this, perhaps, the missing NTN element in many churches and their communities? Are we failing to give proper heed to the call to especially love those in our church?

NTN love of fellow believers, and the world, gave onlookers plenty to talk about. In *The Rise of Christianity*, author Rodney Stark summarizes that in those early centuries after Pentecost, "the Christian way appeared to work." He included a letter written by the pagan emperor Julian to the high priest of Galatia in which Julian complained "that the pagans needed to equal the virtues of Christians, for recent Christian growth was caused by their 'moral character, even if pretended' and by their 'benevolence toward strangers and care for the graves of the dead.'" In a letter to another priest, Julian wrote that while Christians (whom he referred to as "impious Galileans") supported "not only their own poor, but ours as well, everyone can see that our people lack aid from us."[26]

The early church historian Tertullian claimed, "It is our care of the helpless, our practice of loving kindness that brands us in the eyes of many of our opponents. 'Only look,' they say, 'look how they love one another!'"[27]

No one, including the Bible writers, expects a single church to meet every ongoing need of its entire geographic community. Nowhere in recorded history do we see that every financial and physical need in an entire zip code was wiped out just because followers of Jesus happened to set up shop in town. That was not a NTN phenomenon. Neither is it a reasonable expectation now.

But if ever there was a chance to see basic needs for food, clothing, and shelter being met in our communities, Western churches today would arguably have a tremendous shot at it.

Unlike during biblical times, most democratic societies today provide many essential remedies for needy citizens, Christians and non-Christians alike, via significant taxing of the population. A question worth considering is what *basic necessities* meant in New Testament times and what we think it means today. Without the church's financial contribution, most civilized countries today are providing basic necessities at a much higher level, comparatively, than what the early apostles could have hoped or imagined. Whether or not it comes from a generous heart, Christians and non-Christians alike arrive at the table of compassion with a sizeable chunk of their income already "donated" via the tax system. Millions of Americans, for example, "contribute" to the needy every year whenever they write their checks to the IRS.

How would the early church leaders approach the financial needs of citizens who already have access to comprehensive welfare services provided in modern-day Australia, Sweden, or Canada?

Though societal safety nets are far from flawless, it seems that Western churches today should have a much greater ability than the early congregations to make sure every believer's basic needs are met. When unsaved family members and co-workers hear from believers that God is meeting all their needs, it points the way to Jesus. Even more so when the same is said of everyone who goes to that church.

> **When churches operate in this NTN fashion, it creates a positive spiral for far more needy people outside the church to receive help.**

The potential here for maximizing Jesus and having a revolutionary impact on culture is phenomenal. Can we begin to grasp and then unleash the powerful potential of a church that goes above and beyond in showing love for its members? It is okay for *church love* to be deeper and higher and more frequent than *community love*. "Be devoted to one another with brotherly love; … contribute to the needs of the saints, practice hospitality," Paul writes in Romans 12:10, 13. When churches operate in this NTN fashion, it propels the effectiveness of the gospel; it creates a positive spiral where far more needy people *outside* the church receive help than they otherwise would have. Generous churches with giving believers make possible a growing number of ministries that help those trapped in the sex trade, victims of natural disasters, and those lacking adequate food and medical care worldwide.

There is something incredibly attractive (not to mention, newsworthy) about a church where everyone's basic needs are being met. In a healthy, growing church, the once-needy are now increasingly productive and generous, and the self-sufficient are more motivated to give enthusiastically because they routinely see the fruit of their investment. This church is perpetually able to welcome more and more new converts, dealing with the baggage that can accompany individuals and families whose lives have too long operated outside God's paradigms.

And the cycle repeats. More converts come into the kingdom. After a few years, this church has not only brought more people into the family of God for eternity, but they have also truly helped people on a multiplying basis with their basic necessities in a fashion that has potential to be fruit-producing, far-reaching, and long-lasting.

An encouraging trend in U.S. churches has been what foster care advocates term "wrap-around congregations." They recognize that a single family unit is incredibly challenged to provide comprehensive foster care all by themselves. The need is often magnified when there are multiple siblings, special needs, or behavioral issues involved. When a Christian family makes the sacrificial decision to go bring one or more foster care children into their home, their churches are discovering that they have much to give in augmenting this show of Christ's love.

What can the congregation do in support of the adults and couples who have undergone training to be that special home, even in the middle of the night, where the sheriff and social services can safely leave two little boys whose parents were just caught in a serious case of child endangerment? It can train other families in the church to provide ongoing assistance to the foster parents, like a grandma and grandpa "on call." Still other members can help out by becoming certified and opening their homes to the foster child for a week, or weekend, to give the foster parents a needed break.

NTN meant that believers regularly went to these kinds of lengths and more to help one another inside the church. And this enabled them to do more in offering "cups of water in Jesus' name" to the thirsty outside the church, too. It meant they respected their government authorities and fellow citizens and did good to everyone on a routine basis. At one point in the book of Acts, when Judea was wracked by famine, the suffering believers there received help from believers in Antioch (Acts 11:27ff), the extraordinary kind of help many nonbelievers did not presumably receive. Not surprisingly, those followers repetitively found themselves joined by new converts.

Loving one another in this fashion jumpstarts and keeps revving the engine of evangelism and compassion to nonbelievers. Churches who put their oxygen mask on first are being obedient. In addition, they have a far greater ability to provide life-saving and life-changing assistance to nonbelievers in their community who, despite the efforts of family, friends, and government assistance, still find themselves in physical, emotional, or financial need.

Greater unity in this effort would change the public commentary on Christ's church ... which would cause an uptick in effective evangelism. It's happened before. Christians can become known as the people who lovingly take care of one another in such a way that it seems clear to the world that they absolutely love being in each other's company. The sour smell of disunity and strife across the globe these days means it is prime time for the church to distinguish itself with the sweet aroma of the rose among thorns God always intended us to be!

As Paul said to the Thessalonian church, "But we don't need to write to you about the importance of loving each other, for God himself has taught you to love one another. Indeed, you already show your love for all the believers throughout Macedonia. Even so, dear brothers and sisters, we urge you to love them *even more*" (1 Thess. 4:9 NLT).

## GET THE MESSAGE?

As intentional as is the repeated directive to avoid opposing fellow believers in front of the world, the opposite is true when it comes to nonbelievers witnessing the love and care we show one another.

Few commandments are stated more often, by more writers, in more ways across the New Testament than to show to other Christians the kind of love that Christ has shown to us.

Communities of believers who prioritize well-rounded love for one another are employing one of the strongest magnets the church has to attract nonbelievers to the saving knowledge of Jesus Christ.

# SCOLDING'S FUTILITY

Up until this point, our focus has been on communication between believers in two key areas: one that the world should rarely if ever witness, and the other that Jesus wants the whole world to see. We should demonstrate genuine affirmation and support to one another in times of plenty and in times of need, making sure we don't hide that brotherly and sisterly affection from the world.

But when internal offenses and disputes arise, we pivot. It's still love (incredible love, actually), but it's the kind of love that is intentionally employed without drawing the attention of unbelievers. We all prefer gentle, discreet confrontation over public ridicule. Christian disagreement, when handled sloppily, often sends a confusing message to the world—and proves extremely counter-productive to evangelism.

With this chapter, we're zooming in. Our focus shifts to the kind of NTN communication believers have *directly* with nonbelievers. Before we dive in, a few introductory remarks will be helpful.

As in a previous chapter, this one will examine a faulty approach that believers nowadays, like me, seem to have embraced. It will be followed by several chapters outlining what we should do instead if we want to follow NTN principles, and why. I like to know that positive, healthy resolution is coming when I feel like I'm wading through conversations focused on what's going wrong. So hang in there through some potentially challenging pages ahead.

Second, I assume that the reader has heard a steady stream of less-than-optimistic updates about the stagnation or decline of the evangelical church in America and most of the Western world. Most Christ-followers I know have a sense that something is wrong at home.

Meanwhile, reports of rapid church growth across Africa and Asia keep coming. A May 20, 2015, article in the *Washington Post* by Wes Granberg-Michaelson detailed the statistics on U.S. church decline in contrast to the remarkable growth of Christianity worldwide, especially in the Southern Hemisphere.[28] Pew Research's forecast for *The Future of World Religions* (April, 2015) includes the headline that, unless something changes, Christianity will no longer represent a majority of citizens by 2050 in countries such as Australia, France, and the United Kingdom.[29]

I point this out in anticipation of the reaction some are likely to have in the coming paragraphs. Like me, when you ponder these points, you may find yourself saying, "Well, maybe, but what about _____? They took a different approach and it sure seemed to work!" Prominent Christian names and personal acquaintances, past and present, will no doubt come to mind. These are people or stories you may find somewhat exceptional to the principles ahead. But please remind yourself of the prior paragraph when that happens.

Whether you know all the details regarding the particular ministry you might be tempted to highlight in defense of the current state of affairs, ask yourself a question—the same one I have been asking myself: "If that approach was so effective on a broad scale, why haven't we seen better results?" Based on several centuries and more of evidence, can anyone say that the Western church's tactic with nonbelievers is working exceptionally well in our culture?

## Our Strategy on Behavior Modification

So here goes. In our conversations with those who don't know Christ, NTN means we minimize the confrontational talk condemning their politics or choices we deem immoral. Nonbelievers are making harmful decisions in their bedroom, at the bar, in the movie theater, at the ballot box, on their smartphones and computers and, literally, everywhere they go. But the NTN response leads us to prioritize the gospel over issues of morality and politics.

Some readers no doubt heard the "Hallelujah Chorus" just now. For others, *them's fightin' words.* I know. Believe me, I know. I've been fighting with myself for quite some time now.

Doesn't the Bible, especially the New Testament, warn against a litany of sins? Well, yes it does. Isn't there an unmistakable pattern of instruction accompanied by a mountainous pattern of experience indicating it is NTN to warn against lust and sexual immorality of all kinds? Absolutely! In fact, here is a far-from-complete list of discouraged vices, one from each New Testament book starting with Acts:

Acts | *legalism*

Romans | *gossiping*

1 Corinthians | *incest*

2 Corinthians | *jealousy*

Galatians | *hypocrisy*

Ephesians| *drunkenness*

Philippians | *conceit*

Colossians | *fornication*

1 Thess. | *lust*

2 Thess. | *idleness*

1 Timothy | *sodomy*

2 Timothy | *profanity*

Titus | *slander*

Philemon | *slavery*

Hebrews | *adultery*

James | *favoritism*

1 Peter | *grumbling*

2 Peter | *coveting*

1 John | *hatred*

2 John | *deception*

3 John | *malice*

Jude | *flattery*

Rev. | *sexual immorality*

No wonder preachers, teachers, and believers throughout the ages have felt not only justified but compelled to warn everyone about the perils and pitfalls of their transgressions. The Bible declares these practices disobedient to God's law, profoundly harmful in this life, and unfathomably detrimental to eternal life. Further, since all have sinned, there is no believer who cannot testify to the personal pain and past regret of numerous sinful choices. Scripture's teaching, personal remorse, and a Christlike love for others are all powerful motivators for believers to admonish others to cease and desist from sinful practices.

And so we do. Our warnings range from private confrontation in relationships that are extremely close and personal to the broad swipe of preaching to the wicked worldwide. Christian moms and dads daily mourn for teen and adult children running from the Lord, dabbling in or devoting themselves entirely to a variety of unhealthy habits, such as sexual desires and activity outside of marriage God's way. Believing spouses desperately hold out hope that their mate will finally abandon that addiction to abusive substances such as alcohol or drugs.

In millions of Christian families, prayers for deliverance are accompanied by a steady diet of coaxing, pleading, and impassioned arguing for the nonbelieving loved one to forsake their particular sin of choice. For a great number of believing family members, it is infuriating. For others, it is heartbreaking, or at the least confusing and discouraging. For almost all, it is varying shades of embarrassment and exhaustion.

Of course, unhealthy and immoral choices are on magnified display in the nonbelieving culture at large. Sins are not only tolerated, they seem to be celebrated with increasing disregard for the physical and emotional harm that results. To believers with the love and the Word of God inside their hearts, all of this chaos screams, "Do something!" Surely, God doesn't expect us to sit idly by as friends and acquaintances, deceived by the schemes of Satan, fall for the lie that drunkenness is no big deal. Should believers remain quiet when government institutions sanction abortion and same-sex marriage? If we believe in heaven and hell, how could a true child of God not speak out on such destructive and potentially damning behaviors as pornography and prostitution?

This is why the New Testament writers, inspired by God's Holy Spirit, filled their letters with repetitive admonitions to abandon all manner of sin immediately. "The unrighteous shall not inherit the kingdom of God," Paul warns in 1 Corinthians 6:9. Adultery, thievery, and extortion, for example, are not just bad ideas according to this passage, and others. Unrepentant people who practice these sins are actually going to miss heaven. Peter has a similar warning for those who would distort and lie about God's Word (2 Peter 3:14-16). John is right there, too, calling out the lust of the flesh, the lust of the eyes, and the pride of life. They are not of God, and those who embrace these worldly passions will not inherit eternal life (1 John 2:15-17).

We followers of Christ routinely pick up on these themes and re-broadcast them, very often with the purest of intentions. In many ways, our message remains consistent with our New Testament predecessors. Sin destroyed lives two thousand years ago, just as it destroys lives today. Our loving Creator knows what is best for our bodies, our relationships, and our eternal destinies. Anything that separates us from God's best for our souls was to be shunned then just as it should be shunned today. The core of the message is largely unchanged. For centuries, devout Christians have gone to great lengths to warn against the traps and consequences of sin.

So what's the problem as far as NTN communication is concerned?

*The audience.*

In far too many cases, preachers, teachers, and folks in the pews are showing little if any regard for the importance Scripture abundantly places on our *audience.*

## Who's Listening?

If you need a quick refresher, find a Bible with commentary and study notes, and then open each New Testament book from Acts to Revelation. (The four Gospels, too, for that matter). You will be reminded, or perhaps discover for the first time, that all those letters and accounts were written to people who already had Jesus inside them. They were all believers! (Or, at least they claimed to be.) All those warnings against immoral and sinful behaviors? They were leveled directly at the saints, not at the unbelieving world.

Is that news? Is that shocking? (Worse, is this conversation heresy?)

It really shouldn't be, for several reasons. We know that no local church or denomination can claim that its members never struggle with sin. (If you're part of a group like that, here's a hint: run!) From the earliest days of Christ's church until the final moments before the coming kingdom when sin is forever vanquished, misbehaving saints will, in part, characterize the people of God. Not because that's a good or desirable thing. It's because it's a fact thing. A regrettable fact, especially when mature believers stumble, but a fact.

Further, we who love Jesus in the twenty-first century are not alone. As already highlighted, Peter and *even* Barnabas had a sin problem called hypocrisy. In Romans 7:13-25, Paul acknowledged his own sinful struggles, years after he was born again and starting churches. As far as we know, no Christ-followers in the New Testament, and none since then, have lived sin-free, before or after salvation. Still, any fair reading of the New Testament leaves us concluding that sin should be avoided like the plague.

Which is why we are also confident God's Spirit possesses all the necessary power to help us overcome every sin. There is always a way out of every temptation (1 Corinthians 10:13). But Scripture and human experience also prepare us for the likelihood of our ongoing challenges with overcoming sin. Consequently, as long as we are breathing on this planet, we will need to ask forgiveness, because sin-free perfection has not been achieved this side of heaven, with the notable exception of our Lord.

Jesus Himself made it clear there are at least two things His disciples needed routinely: food and forgiveness. When one of the Twelve asked Jesus to teach on prayer, His iconic result included, "Give us *this day* our daily bread. And forgive us our debts, as we forgive our debtors" (Matt. 6:11). We are hungry daily. Most of us sin daily. And most of us are sinned against daily.

For emphasis, after Jesus finished the model prayer, He immediately clarified that we need to forgive others of their trespasses freely (vv. 14-15). In part, that act of granting forgiveness influences how our heavenly Father forgives *our* trespasses. Freely forgiving = freely forgiven. Hardly forgiving = hardly forgiven. Again, this is the response given to a disciple, a close follower of Jesus. The next time your stomach reminds you that it is time for food, you might want to check whether it's also time to ask for, and freely give, forgiveness!

Lest we become depressed and defeated, the New Testament clarifies that there is a big difference between daily sins and a life devoted to a sinful lifestyle. First John 5:16-17 speaks of sins that don't lead to death, as opposed to allegiance to sin, which does. While ultimately God alone is the one who knows our heart and its motivations, the condition of all the redeemed is to be continually forgiven with mercies that are (thank God!) new every morning.

Granted, heaven and earth are filled with countless, legitimate testimonies of utter deliverance from sin. Alcoholics who encountered Christ and never took another drop, even claiming to not have the desire. Sexually addicted men and women who, through the power of the gospel, overcame their forgiven past and went on to enjoy healthy, long-lasting marriages.

But every born-again alcoholic or porn star soon discovers, sometimes unexpectedly, that anger and hatred are awfully nasty temptations, too. Drug dealers and bank robbers can get saved, only to find out their uncontrolled arrogance is more of a problem than they knew. Millions of believers who don't necessarily have a dramatic personal story still find it a daily grind to control their tongue and their sexual impulses. All have sinned. All have sinful issues and desires hidden from others and even from themselves but which are fully known by God.

The process of a believer daily becoming more like Christ through the Spirit's power (Paul calls this "sanctification") is somewhat like peeling back the layers of an onion. If on Day One of our salvation God laid us out by revealing every single sinful aspect of our nature, it would be too much to bear. (Not to mention, it would take too much time!) Thankfully, it is not too great a task for God to forgive us immediately of every sin (which He promises He does), whether word or thought or deed. From the moment we repent and cry out for mercy through the sacrifice of Jesus, our whole onion is saved and on its way to heaven. But along the way, God's Spirit gently peels back and peels off the multiple layers of sin—many that we knew were there, and many that were previously hidden for one reason or another.

This is both good news and bad news simultaneously, with the good far outweighing the bad. Yes, it's bad news: the 90-year-

> **Should we be preaching and teaching about sin? More or less. Quite possibly, more AND less.**

old saint still has issues with selfishness and immorality. But there's good news, too—actually, *great* news! That saint was completely forgiven and is daily being completely forgiven as she forgives others and asks God for His continual mercy. The believer who routinely prays and repents will have fewer and fewer sinful hang-ups (onion layers), because the Holy Spirit is able to alter the desires of the heart that delights in the things of God (Psalm 37:4). It's a benefit of the other part of the prayer Jesus encouraged: "Lead us not into temptation, but deliver us from evil." Think about this and gratefully smile through the tears the next time you peel that onion.

So, where does that leave us with our audience? Should NTN believers be preaching and teaching about sin? More or less. Quite possibly, more *and* less. We need more communication (arguably, more than ever) to fellow believers about living moral lives and avoiding the devastation that sinful lifestyles always deliver. James 5:20 gives just one example, highlighting our need to turn a sinning brother "from the error of his way." But less of the same when knowingly speaking to someone who has not yielded their life to the lordship of Jesus Christ. Believers who berate, rebuke, and debate with nonbelievers over their individual immoral choices have little, if any, biblical basis for their approach.

There is, for sure, a critical difference between embracing morality and embracing Christ as Savior. The preaching in the

New Testament required preachers and believers to challenge and sometimes debate with nonbelievers about their choices and sins related to the heart of the gospel. Are you worshiping another God, either through idolatry or sorcery? Are you refusing to acknowledge Christ as the Messiah, including His death and resurrection? Get ready! You are a prime candidate, according to the pattern of Scripture, to be directly confronted about that by a born-again child of God, operating in gracious love and obedience.

But, it bears repeating: There are no examples from Acts to Revelation showing the early church leaders confronting *non*believers about their immorality or their political leanings. When you read their letters, they direct their warnings about immorality solely to the household of faith. When you examine all of the encounters with nonbelievers in the book of Acts (covered in detail in the next chapter), you don't find a *single* reference to believers debating nonbelievers about their sexual practices or their consumption of harmful substances. The NTN focus on sharing warnings about immorality, whether by preaching, admonishing, or rebuking, was in the context of an audience of believers.

### Why We Do What We Do

Clearly, we in the Western church are choosing a different approach. There is overwhelming evidence today of Christians robustly challenging and condemning nonbelievers for their immoral behavior or their political preferences. Why?

Well, for one reason, television, radio, online publications, and social media provide expanding and accessible means for calling out nonbelievers (and, unfortunately, fellow believers, too, as we have already examined). This includes people we know, often family, as well as countless masses we've never even been in the same room with.

There are also more nonbelievers and believers today, along with more stories of misbehavior, so the sheer opportunity for this dynamic is greater than ever.

Third, in many Western nations, the church and state are no longer in as much agreement about what constitutes sin. In the United States and many nations, behaviors long viewed sinful by the church were similarly viewed by the main branches of government. Though previously outlawed, it is now no longer a crime, for example, to commit most forms of adultery or abortion. Many other examples could be cited, including the relatively recent additions of marrying someone of the same sex or walking freely into a public restroom when your gender at birth does not match the gender icon on the door.

"The world is going to hell in a handbasket," we often hear. Many seasoned saints grew up in a time of regular campaigning against cigarettes, beer, lottery tickets, and girlie magazines, all of which were—and still are—far too available at the local convenience store. Consequently, the ongoing multiplication of moral vices is very unsettling to believers who feel desperate to reverse culture's downward spiral.

If, somehow, it is actually true that the New Testament lacks any specific examples of Christians condemning nonbelievers over their moral choices, are there any possible explanations that would justify us following a different path? A lot has changed in two thousand years. And, they did live in the *"Holy" Land* after all. Maybe the widespread sins of the twenty-first century weren't as prevalent back then?

Hardly! Both the Old Testament and New Testament attest that believers and nonbelievers alike fell prey to wide varieties of sinful behaviors. The list of New Testament books that opened this chapter makes that point clear. Everywhere the apostles went as they spread the gospel message, whether in Judea or in Gentile areas heavily influenced by Greco-Roman culture, sins did very much abound. Many of these we would sadly but easily recognize today, such as theft and lying and sexually abusing minors. But there were also those that are rather foreign to our modern understanding.

The brutality and murder that were on display for sport and sheer entertainment in the gladiator coliseums form just one example. They weren't just tolerated, they were celebrated. There was also widespread slavery. It is commonly estimated by historians today that much of the population of Rome lived in slavery, some say one out of every five persons. Others indicate ratios much higher. By comparison, a *Washington Post* article cited the country of Mauritania on the African continent as having the world's highest rate of slavery today: "only" one in twenty-five.[30] Ancient Rome and many other places in the Middle East had a very serious slave problem, as evidenced in Paul's writings.

Further, not only was abortion common, so was infanticide. Parents were

> Of the many acts of the apostles recorded by Luke, not one included debating with community movers and shakers about prevalent injustices.

known to abandon live born babies, a practice called "exposure," leaving the young, defenseless child to starve to death unless they perished sooner at the hands of the elements or wild animals. In the face of immense financial and societal hardships, some parents felt they could not afford to raise more than one or two children, so males with disabilities and females in general were often undesirable. In *Backgrounds of Early Christianity*, Everett Ferguson notes, "A papyrus from Egypt, notable for its date (1 B.C.) as well as for its contents, illustrates the pagan attitude. Hilarion writes from Alexandria to his wife Alis at home in the interior: "I beg and entreat you, take care of the little one, and as soon as we receive our pay I will send it up to you. If by chance you bear a child, if it is a boy, let it be; if it is a girl, expose it."[31]

Sin and immorality were indisputably rampant then, and unfathomably evil, as they are now. No one questions that. So why are there no New Testament reports of believers rebuking nonbelievers for their immoral lifestyles? No patterns at all.

Is this line of thought deeply troubling or perplexing to you, as it was to me? How could Paul and Peter and the other apostles be so silent with their unbelieving audiences? In all of their letters, they didn't include a single instruction for believers to challenge or confront nonbelievers about their immoral behaviors. Neither did they provide any examples of how they themselves rebuked nonbelievers for their sinful practices with money, sex, and intoxicating substances. Moreover, we read of no pleas for pagan leaders to end society's disrespectful treatment of women, children, the elderly, and the disadvantaged. Of the many acts of the apostles recorded by Luke, not one of those acts included debating with community movers and shakers about prevalent injustices. Didn't they care about all the atrocities happening around them? Didn't God care?

## Citizenship Matters

The New Testament view of citizenship is central at this point. By birth or by choice, nearly every human being is a citizen of some country on the globe. Varying degrees of privileges and responsibilities are attached to every individual's citizenry based on their locale. Even in the same country, there can be variances in what is expected by and provided for the citizens of one state or one municipality, compared to others. All human behavior is influenced in some measure by both the freedoms and demands of citizenry.

As the apostle Peter explains, born-again believers are actually "aliens and refugees" here on planet Earth, with our citizenship firmly established in heaven (1 Peter 2:11). Even if we have passports in the nation of our birth, Christians understand the preeminence of our heavenly citizenry, appropriately captured in the old country gospel lyric "This world is not my home, I'm just passing through ... If heaven's not my home, then Lord what will I do?"

The list of game-changing benefits that come with being a citizen of heaven also have their share of requirements. As Christ-followers, we recognize that we have a responsibility to love God with our whole heart and to love our neighbors as ourselves. We jeopardize our citizen status in heaven if we reject God and His commands. This is why we need countless sermons and Bible studies and prayer sessions to make sure we are keeping up on our end of the best bargain in the history of the world. We should thank God when pastors and teachers and evangelists step on our toes in the spiritual sense. Our heavenly citizenry is too much to risk losing because our hearts turned cold to God's guidelines for holy living.

But hear this: Our unbelieving friends have no such citizenry (yet). The devastating news is that they are bound for eternity separated from God, and yes, there will be weeping and gnashing of teeth.

In exchange, however, God hardly expects (nor should we) that foreigners would accept the responsibilities of a heavenly citizenship. Though it is not His desire, God anticipates that nonbelievers will regularly commit many sins in direct violation of spiritual law, because they are not yet citizens of the kingdom. As Brady Boyd, a Colorado pastor, sometimes puts it, "Dogs bark; cats meow; sinners sin!"

Appropriately, earthly governments and fellow countrymen (including Christians) will expect people to avoid unlawful behavior, such as committing murder. This is true whether or not they are Christians (or Jews or Muslims or Hindus or atheists, for that matter). Why? Because murder violates the law of the land. Because the benefits that come with our earthly citizenship are tied to expectations. With few exceptions, wherever murderers reside, they will go to jail or even be put to death for shedding innocent blood. Their citizenship has requirements, such as being punished for criminal acts.

> We have to admit that telling people whose hearts are not surrendered to Jesus to "Stop it!" rarely seems to work.

But when we admonish nonbelievers to change other behaviors that happen to be legal, without first changing their citizenry, it doesn't work. We are, in effect, attempting to rebuild the old system of the law from which Christ set us free. We are often attempting to coerce them to do something they are not required to do, and which they lack the scriptural and moral compass to fully grasp.

This is often difficult for passionate believers to comprehend. "Seriously? Why is it so hard for them to understand that living and sleeping together outside of marriage can have devastating consequences? Why do our next-door neighbors think it's okay to constantly indulge with drugs and alcohol?" As we would have to admit, telling people whose hearts are not surrendered to Jesus to "Stop it!" (whatever *it* is) rarely seems to work. Especially for the long term, which matters most.

Christians have supposedly moved past the law. Paul masterfully captures the futility of trying to live by laws without Christ in our hearts in Galatians 2:15-21 (NLT).

You and I are Jews by birth, not "sinners" like the Gentiles. Yet we know that a person is made right with God by faith in Jesus Christ, not by obeying the law. And we have believed in Christ Jesus, so that we might be made right with God because of our faith in Christ, not because we have obeyed the law. For no one will ever be made right with God by obeying the law.

But suppose we seek to be made right with God through faith in Christ and then we are found guilty because we have abandoned the law. Would that mean Christ has led us into sin? Absolutely not! Rather, I am a sinner if I rebuild the old system of law I already tore down. For when I tried to keep the law, it condemned me. So I died to the law—I stopped trying to meet all its requirements—so that I might live for God. My old self has been crucified with Christ. It is no longer I who live, but Christ lives in me. So I live in this earthly body by trusting in the Son of God, who loved me and gave himself for me. I do not treat the grace of God as meaningless. For if keeping the law could make us right with God, then there was no need for Christ to die.

Several years ago, I voluntarily became a member, a "citizen" of sorts, of a local gym. Perhaps you know the drill I went through, especially if regular exercise has mysteriously eluded your calendar for years (okay, decades!). Though I definitely felt like a foreigner as I joined, I quickly discovered that a fair share of enjoyable rights accompanied my new membership, *along with* some challenging responsibilities.

I gained access to thousands of dollars of equipment I could have never purchased, stored, or maintained on my own. Trainers have motivated and coached me to lose weight and shape up. But I have to do my part. It is my responsibility to be more disciplined with my diet. I have to do my own exercises outside the gym and then show up on time for scheduled appointments. Sadly, I have to admit I was previously not up for those kinds of responsibilities, until I joined and experienced some of the benefits.

While I have much to work on before achieving additional goals, I have undoubtedly benefited from my membership thus far. One of the key components that makes me smile, and which encourages me to keep working, is the training I receive.

Every week, without fail, I am learning entirely new exercises, even after all this time. They are often variations for targeting the same area of the body. But the equipment setting, or the positioning, or the range of motion is something I actually never tried before, at least that way.

I frequently laugh at myself whenever I realize that my clunky coordination is not getting any better with age. But I love it! The new exercises keep me on my toes, create some healthy pain, and remind me I've still got much to learn and master.

How much more when people join the ranks of the redeemed! We cannot expect foreigners who don't yet belong to adopt the responsibilities of heavenly citizenry. In fact, we can't even expect outright citizens to do so when they are new believers. It takes time (in my case, a lifetime) to fully understand all the ways our behaviors and attitudes need to align with our Creator's master design. The apostle James in Acts 15 confirms this approach when he specifically admonishes new Gentile believers to "abstain … from sexual immorality" (v. 29). Is it by pure accident that the New Testament captures no such apostolic instruction to Gentiles *before* they are saved?

So, the NTN pattern of experience on this topic is, actually, the absence of one. The pattern is that there are no examples to cite. There are no stories of disciples showing us how to debate issues of morality or political persuasions with a nonbeliever. They simply didn't do it.

By contrast, the pattern of instruction is on full display. Romans, 1 Corinthians, and Hebrews, among other sections, add to the theme cited above in Galatians. They all underscore the concept that challenging the morality of a nonbeliever is unwise and ill-advised. It's putting the cart before the horse.

- When you [Jewish and Gentile believers in Rome] say they [pagans] are wicked and should be punished, you are condemning yourself, for you who judge others do these very same things [such as boasting, coveting, and being sexually immoral]. (Romans 2:1 NLT)

- But the natural man does not receive the things of the Spirit of God, for they are foolishness to him; nor can he know them, because they are spiritually discerned. [This is why Paul said in this same chapter that he came to the Corinthians at first simply preaching Christ crucified.] (1 Corinthians 2:14)

- But solid food belongs to those who are of full age, that is, those who by reason of use have their senses exercised to discern both good and evil. [This is meant to contrast mature believers with new believers. And if even new believers can't easily discern good from evil, why would we expect nonbelievers to be able to do so?] (Hebrews 5:14)

- So I say, let the Holy Spirit guide your lives. Then you won't be doing what your sinful nature craves. The sinful nature wants to do evil, which is just the opposite of what the Spirit wants. And the Spirit gives us desires that are the opposite of what the sinful nature desires. [It can be argued, both in theory and practice, that pleading or "guilting" nonbelievers into good behavior is destined to fail. Without the Holy Spirit guiding their lives, which Paul claims to be an essential component for people who are already saved, nonbelievers will likely keep doing what their sinful nature craves.] (Galatians 5:16-17 NLT)

Can't you just hear the Apostle Paul saying, "Don't make me come back there and tell you what I already told you!" There are other passages supporting this line of instruction as well.

This is not at all to say that a believer wearing some type of recognized authority hat shouldn't use that influence to steer nonbelievers toward moral choices. In addition to setting a positive example (the most effective preaching we can do), parents and bosses and teachers, for example, need to act. They must speak out. Parents should do and say everything within their power to influence a child to abstain from immoral behavior, and the sooner the better. That's a parent's freedom and, Scripture would indicate, a parent's responsibility. All societies are utterly dependent on parents, whatever their faith, to skillfully steer their children toward moral choices. Christian parents should lead the way and set the example in this regard. To their chagrin at times, my own children have frequently heard from me about moral and political choices.

Similarly, a born-again person wearing the hat of a boss or coworker should absolutely speak to a coworker about immoral behavior that affects the company. Warn, help, or possibly expose and fire the employee who keeps stealing from the company. Fellow citizens are empowered and expected in many cases to speak up when illegal activities are taking place. The key question is, "What hat are we wearing, and what hat is our audience wearing?" Depending on the context, quoting Scripture in the process of encouraging morality may or may not be prudent, effective, or even permitted.

But when the most obvious hat we are wearing in a particular situation is "I'm simply a Christ-follower, representing God and His people," and the most obvious hat our audience is wearing is "I'm not a follower of Christ and I'm, therefore, not under your spiritual or moral authority," debates about morality and politics are to be avoided. Instead, the gospel presentation should take front and center. This is the scenario found repeatedly in Scripture.

## Scolding Doesn't Work

Unfortunately, too many moral or political debates with unbelievers are being pursued by too many believers today. For some, the pursuit may be unwitting. Perhaps the believer assumes that everyone in his or her audience is a believer when sounding off about a politician's immoral choices. But the audience can often be larger and more diverse than imagined. If someone goes on Facebook to post an article on why any consumption of alcohol is sinful and harmful, citing Scripture for support, there's no guarantee that many who are unsaved won't see it.

For other believers, their sense of legitimate frustration sadly yields to illegitimate expression. "Somebody's got to say something!" they scream inside (or maybe even outside on occasion). "Our culture, our young people … they desperately need to know that _____ is such a harmful choice. It will bring them so much pain in the long run and will, quite possibly, rob them of the healthy, productive life they were designed by their Creator to live." Yes, indeed; the New Testament repeatedly warns that lifestyle choices can become traps that lead to eternal separation from God. With the stakes so consequential, we feel the urge to speak out, knowing full well that one or more members of our audience have no relationship with Jesus. "What Christian, in their right mind, would withhold the truth from the people who need to hear it the most?" we say to ourselves.

The early church felt that way too. But their focus was on the truth of the gospel. If our desire is to see people set free from the sins that enslave them and bring such harm to their loved ones, we owe it to them and to ourselves to follow the pattern of the apostles. How did they see scores of people set free from sexual deviation? How were addicts delivered again and again? It wasn't due to Christian meddling in the private lives of nonbelievers. Paul emphasized this with the Thessalonians: "Make it your goal to live a quiet life, minding your own business" (1 Thess. 4:11 NLT). Instead, the disciples preached about Jesus. They spoke about Jesus. Facing the risk of their personal safety, they taught about Jesus, and then taught about Jesus some more.

Not everyone who heard God's plan for salvation through the risen Messiah believed. But oh so many did! And once they were born again, they were baptized in water, they were baptized in the Holy Spirit—and *then* they were instructed over and over again about the wages of sin. Forgiven of their sins, healed from years of despair and hurt, the hope of eternal life grew inside their spirits and provided good soil for the truth about right and wrong behavior to finally take hold. These new believers could readily see it in the church leaders. They observed mature fellow believers living differently than the world, with a deep peace that seemed so strange and appealing compared to the anxiety of unbelievers. The precepts about lifestyle choices that once seemed so foreign now seemed less so.

Not only did the early church talk about Jesus, they showed the love of Jesus. This is a good place to draw a needed distinction between rebuking the offender and helping the offended. While we may find it hard to convince a pimp, on moral grounds, to give up the disgusting amount of money he is making off the sex trade, Christians are finding it increasingly doable to show Christ's love to his victims. People who have been hurt and wounded by the immoral choices of others need tangible demonstrations of our love. What a God-honoring way to show compassion and, often, to help a victim find not only physical and emotional healing but eternal life through Jesus.

This is not to discount the testimonies of saints who point to a conversation, a sermon, a TV or radio program, a pamphlet, or even a website that confronted them about a particular sin, and this became the turning point that led them to the Lord. "I was a drunken, foul-mouthed partier when a Christian co-worker confronted me about my offensive behavior. That was thirty years ago, and here I am today, serving the Lord!" Or "I had an abortion and saw a pamphlet explaining how displeasing it is to God to take an innocent life. I turned to God that day and have been walking in forgiveness and healing ever since!"

I am not seeking to disqualify such testimonies. To the contrary! Believers always celebrate any story of someone being unshackled from the weight of sin and walking in right relationship with God. I simply want to acknowledge two irrefutable facts. (1) The pattern of instruction and experience in the New Testament shows us that when the disciples spoke with nonbelievers, they focused on the gospel, not their moral choices. (2) No Christian leaders or churches today, especially in Western culture, would describe our kingdom advances as rivaling or approaching the evangelistic success of the early church. Hence, it is not so much that rebuking a nonbeliever about his gambling addiction is always wrong as much as we're always right to keep our conversations with nonbelievers focused on the gospel.

That is what Paul emphasized continually. He gave his energies to preaching Christ. Listen to his declaration in Colossians 1:27-29 (NKJV). "... Christ in you, the hope of glory. Him we preach, warning every man and teaching every man in all wisdom, that we may present every man perfect in Christ Jesus. To this end I also labor, striving according to His working which works in me mightily."

Paul goes to lengths in Romans 7 to explain the futility of preaching moral codes instead of the gospel. Before Christ enters our hearts, our sinful nature is so twisted. The sin inside us takes our good attempts (such as trying to obey the whole law) and uses that to stir up rebellion, so we keep sinning even more. Now think about that in the present context. When good people (Christians) take a good thing (a warning about sin) and try applying it to a heart without Christ inside, the well-intentioned warning often has the opposite effect of what was intended. Have you found that to be true? Instead of saying, "Why, thank you for warning me about pornography. I believe I will stop using it forever," the addict without Christ in his heart has little chance of gaining victory in this area. Sin inside a Christless heart is ferociously self-preserving. It repeatedly twists and distorts any reasonable and godly counsel that threatens its control.

Paul's explanation here comes to the frustrated Christian as a dual messenger of relief and admonition. If you are exasperated or brokenhearted that a loved one without Christ continues in their harmful lifestyle, despite your many pleas to forsake those habits, there's a reason. It's not your lack of passion or persuasive abilities. Their true need is Jesus. Your biggest concern should be that they invite Jesus to reside and reign. In the meantime, harping on a particular sin is not the answer.

In fact, Paul concludes Romans 7 by underscoring that Jesus is the answer for the Christian too. As a saved believer and preacher of the gospel, Paul admits that he himself has still struggled with various sins. In many ways, Paul still considered his heart enslaved to sin. But was he depressed? If there were no remedy, perhaps. But that was not the case. Thank God! Paul said. The answer is in Jesus Christ our Lord.

He continued the victory march in chapter 8, by adding that it is God's Spirit dwelling inside us that gives us hope and power to win the battle over sin, daily and for eternity. "But if through the power of the Spirit you put to death the deeds of your sinful nature, you will live" (Romans 8:13 NLT). This is all great news and worthy of many sermons and books that have been written on the subject. For our purposes in this chapter, it only cements the truth that those still living apart from God are actually helpless to change their sinful minds.

## Lighting the Way

Manipulating and pressuring are human weapons, used for centuries. Shouting. Fighting with words, with fists, with threats. Christians don't employ those kind of weapons. Instead, they turn to faith-filled prayer and intercession, spiritual gifts, anointed preaching, Scripture memorization, humbling ourselves, and taking time to sincerely listen and build genuine relationships so God's love can shine. For anyone interested in seeing people saved and turn from their harmful lifestyles, this is the way to go. Paul draws the comparison this way: "For though we walk in the flesh, we do not war according to the flesh. For the weapons of our warfare are not carnal, but mighty through God to the pulling down of strongholds, casting down imaginations and every high thing that exalts itself against the knowledge of God, bringing every thought into captivity to the obedience of Christ" (2 Cor. 10:3-5).

What are carnal ways to try to pull down strongholds? Pressure. Ridicule. Nagging. Paul makes another telling comparison between those who pressure for a particular behavior and those who focus on Christ: "Those who are trying to force you to be circumcised want to look good to others. They don't want to be persecuted for teaching that the cross of Christ alone can save" (Gal. 6:12 NLT). Based on social pressure, Judaizers were transferring social pressure onto others. How far from the gospel!

Is the tool you're using to talk to someone about their morals a human tool or a heavenly one? Never-ending debates … threatening … berating … begging … patronizing—doesn't that list make you weary? God has a better way, empowering you to win the battle *and* the war if your messaging stays focused on surrendering to Christ.

Paul expounds on this better way in Ephesians. He explains that the light of Christ in us is the way to expose the evil works of the world. How do we show how harmful and evil adultery is? First of all, we avoid committing adultery ourselves! We walk in righteousness in our marriages and raising our children. How do we paint the clearest picture that gambling can be devastating? We allow the light of Christ to shine through our financial practices, as we cheerfully give to the work of the Lord and avoid foolish spending. We expose immoral habits and their devastation by the light of Jesus inside us!

Consider this pattern of instruction for letting our light shine:

- For you were once darkness, but now you are light in the Lord. Walk as children of light (for the fruit of the Spirit is in all goodness, righteousness, and truth), finding out what is acceptable to the Lord. And have no fellowship with the unfruitful works of darkness, but rather expose them. For it is shameful even to speak of those things which are done by them in secret. But all things that are exposed are made manifest by the light, for whatever makes manifest is light. Therefore He says: "Awake, you who sleep, Arise from the dead, and Christ will give you light." (Ephesians 5:8-14 NKJV)
- Arise, shine, for your light has come, and the glory of the Lord has risen upon you. For the darkness shall cover the earth and deep darkness the peoples; but the Lord shall rise upon you, and His glory shall be seen upon you. The nations shall come to your light and kings to the brightness of your rising. (Isaiah 60:1-3)
- Let your light so shine before men that they may see your good works and glorify your Father who is in heaven. (Matthew 5:16)

In the next chapter, we celebrate the key method used by the early church to let their lights shine. They told anyone who would listen about Jesus!

# GET THE MESSAGE?

Whatever may be right or wrong with the approach of the stagnant or declining church in Western societies, no one questions the impressive growth, by comparison, of Christianity across many parts of Africa and Asia where believers routinely preach Jesus without publicly pushing nonbelievers for moral or political change.

Following the example of New Testament leaders means we should prioritize the gospel in our conversations with those who don't know Christ while minimizing the confrontational talk condemning their politics or immorality.

Throughout the New Testament, the abundant, explicit, and repetitive warnings about immoral behavior are directed exclusively to the people of God, not toward pagan unbelievers.

In heaven's warfare against sin, believers choose mighty weapons like declaring the truth about Jesus and allowing His light to shine through us rather than using carnal weapons like pressuring, ridicule, and endless debates.

# 7

# WHAT'S MOST IMPORTANT?

The patterns of instruction and experience in Acts and the rest of the New Testament make a compelling case for focusing our preaching and teaching among nonbelievers on the "gospel of the kingdom." This phrase shows up repeatedly— at the beginning of Jesus' ministry (Matt. 4:23; Mark 1:15), in the middle (Matt. 9:35), and near the end (Matt. 24:14). His followers would hardly have thought about preaching or teaching anything else.

The Gospel writers Matthew and Mark close their books with the Great Commission, in which Jesus commanded the eleven remaining disciples to make disciples of all nations: "Go into all the world and preach the gospel" (Mark 16:15). Jesus added that gospel preachers should expect confirming signs such as speaking in tongues, divine protection, and healing the sick. Luke fills his second book (Acts) with one story after another of the disciples faithfully fulfilling Christ's commandment and then experiencing firsthand the very signs of confirmation He promised.

So what exactly is "the gospel"? When we preach and teach the gospel (literally translated, *good news*), we are explaining God's good news about His kingdom. That God has always wanted eternal fellowship and communion with His creation. That Adam's sin brought a horrible and universal estrangement in that relationship. That this rift cannot be mended by the law or by human effort, but only by the sacrifice of God's only begotten Son, Jesus Christ, on the cross, who was raised from the dead three days later. That this Jesus is the promised Messiah foretold by the prophets throughout the Old Testament. That, no matter our sinful past, all we have to do—and all we can do—is repent and receive by faith the free gift of forgiveness, God's amazing grace. That all who refuse Christ will be separated from God for eternity in the lake of fire, called hell. That hell wasn't created for us but for a rebellious angel, Lucifer (Satan), and his demons, who use whatever means necessary to deceive humans, keeping them blind to God's truth. But that all who accept Christ as their Savior and who serve the Lord, while far from perfect, are forgiven and washed clean in God's eyes because of the shed blood of Christ. That they have the assurance of the Holy Spirit's presence and power as they live for Christ here on earth. That they are on their way to eternal life in a new heaven and earth, free of sin and pain, spectacular beyond our imagination.

The first instruction to preach the gospel, then, comes from Jesus Christ Himself: Win nonbelievers to the kingdom by prioritizing the gospel. Turn nonbelievers into disciples. Just as Peter, James, John, and the others became disciples when Jesus called them to "Follow me," Christ admonished them to invite others to follow Him, too.

But they weren't to stop there. "Baptize them," Jesus said, "and teach them to observe all things I have commanded you" (Matt. 28:19-20). This chronology is not accidental, and it is critical: (1) Get them saved. (2) Get them baptized. (3) Teach them how to follow Christ.

Paul added to the pattern of instruction about gospel prioritization. He reminded the believers in Corinth that the very first and most important thing he preached to them was the gospel: "that Christ died for our sins according to the Scriptures, and that He was buried, and that He rose again the third day according to the Scriptures" (1 Corinthians 15:3-4 NKJV). 1 Corinthians 1:17-18 and Colossians 1:27-29 are other passages leaving no question that Paul fully embraced his Savior's passion for sticking to the core gospel.

## A Parable

Melvin was so frustrated. Slamming the door with one hand while the other carried his towel-covered bucket, he stormed into the house. Entering the kitchen, he muttered to his wife, Marge, that he was thinking about never going fishing anymore. "I give up! They're impossible to clean, you know that?" Nothing had gone right that day, apparently.

"Well, my goodness! What happened out there?" she asked.

"I don't know! I thought I'd start by cutting along their undersides, you know, to gut them."

"Yeah? Well, let me have a look at them," Marge offered encouragingly.

"That didn't work at all," he replied. "So, I thought a different angle might work. I tried cutting off their heads, but that didn't do the trick either, so I moved to their tails."

"They can't be *that* bad. Let me see that bucket," she said, reaching out. By now, she was becoming very curious.

"No!" he said, yanking the bucket away. "I finally tried slicing off a few scales but, I'm telling you, it was impossible!"

She suddenly noticed bloody bandages on several fingers. "Melvin, what did you do to yourself? Let me see that bucket!" And, with that, she managed to yank away the towel ... only to discover that the bucket was completely empty.

"Melvin! I don't understand. Why did you throw all those fish away?"

"Throw them away?" he shot back. "I would never throw fish away, Marge. I just didn't catch any."

And it *never* gets any easier trying to clean fish we haven't yet caught.

In reality, fish not only have to be caught. It helps when they're good and dead. Of course, you don't want them to be dead too long before you start cleaning them.

I know I'm setting the table here to be terribly quoted out of context, but it's true: Dead sinners are much easier to work with—spiritually dead, of course. Once the old, sinful self is dead and buried (as beautifully symbolized by water baptism), we are raised to walk in newness of life. When things are squared with Jesus, and His righteous blood starts flowing through our veins, the shedding of past habits has a much better shot at happening naturally. How *super*natural!

Jesus purposefully painted the word picture for us when He told His disciples He planned to make them "fishers of men" (Matt. 4:19). His goal was that we would grasp the full analogy about fishing. Skilled fishermen know how to approach, capture, and *then* clean their fish, in that order.

Any other sequence is doomed from the outset, as Melvin painfully discovered.

### Gospel First

Adding to this pattern of instruction are further insights about the purpose of preaching the gospel to nonbelievers before anything else. These include passages addressed in the previous chapter, such as 1 Corinthians 2 and Hebrews 5. And doesn't it make a tremendous amount of sense to do it this way? What is most striking, repetitive, and apparently overlooked in the New Testament is that the preachers and teachers of Acts strictly prioritized the gospel when speaking with nonbelievers.

It is critical to note that the term *nonbelievers* underwent a radical shift after the Day of Pentecost. Prior to Christ's sacrifice and resurrection, the children of God had included those who devoutly worshiped Him and followed the Law, offering repeated sacrifices to atone for their sins. After Christ became the only sacrifice required in God's eyes, those who rejected Christ's sacrifice as God's atonement for their sins were no longer on their way to heaven, even if they still faithfully practiced the Law.

Admittedly, this is a very curious question, and one that is relevant to this whole discussion on several levels. First, as mentioned above, it impacts the timeframe associated with the shift of membership in God's family.

> **Skilled fishermen know how to approach, capture, and *then* clean their fish, in that order.**

Were the requirements for salvation altered after Christ began His preaching ministry? What happened to the Samaritan woman or those in her village (see John 4) who, by definition, did not follow all the Jewish laws? Apparently, she and many of her friends believed wholeheartedly that Christ was the Messiah. What if, a few months later, some of these followers died before Christ was crucified? Were they children of God? We would assume so.

But wasn't the atoning work of the Lamb completed *after* Christ's crucifixion? Maybe it was actually after the resurrection? Or perhaps our patient heavenly Father waited until after the birth of the church on Pentecost? The answer, of course, is up to God. He knows exactly when He wants things to happen in an effort to redeem as many as possible.

To the current point, is it true that disciples in the New Testament concentrated their conversations with nonbelievers on the Good News? As we have previously affirmed, all the books and letters in the New Testament were written by a believer to another believer or a group of believers.

But in the book of Acts in particular, as recorded by Luke the physician, we see one example after another of believers interacting with unbelieving Jews and Gentiles alike. In more than three dozen recorded stories about Peter, Paul, and other church leaders addressing nonbelievers in the book of Acts, we find them consistently speaking in some way about the gospel of the kingdom. They *never once* engaged in a conversation for the sole purpose of identifying the nonbelievers' particular sin, unless the sin was rejecting Christ. There's no direct mention *anywhere* of confronting pagans about their adultery, fornication, drunkenness, homosexuality, abortion, slavery, or lust. Clearly, all of these were fair game, as they were certainly issues of the day. Idol worship was condemned, but that particular sin goes to the heart of the gospel thrust: Only Jesus, not false gods, can save!

It takes just a couple of hours to read through Acts in one sitting. I encourage you to do it as soon as you can. For now, here is a quick summary of each episode in which believers spoke directly with nonbelievers:

1. To the Jewish foreigners at Pentecost in Acts 2, Peter declared that God made Jesus our resurrected Lord and Savior, and was now sending His Holy Spirit to empower disciples to spread the Good News.

2. To the lame man at the temple gate in chapter 3, Peter said, "In the name of Jesus Christ of Nazareth, rise up and walk," and the man was instantly healed.

3. To the Jewish onlookers at Solomon's Porch in chapter 3, Peter urged repentance to enjoy refreshing from the presence of the Lord.

4. To the Jewish rulers of the Sanhedrin, who were greatly disturbed that the apostles were preaching resurrection through Christ in chapter 4, Peter declared there is no other name but Jesus by which we must be saved.

5. To those same Jewish rulers of the Sanhedrin in chapter 5 who reprimanded them for teaching people about Jesus, Peter asserted that God raised up Jesus to be Prince and Savior.

6. To the people of Jerusalem in chapter 5, the apostles did not cease teaching and preaching eternal life through Jesus Christ, performing many miracles in His name.

7. To the Jewish rulers of the Sanhedrin who eventually stoned Stephen in chapter 7, he boldly accused their fathers of killing those who foretold of the coming Messiah, whom they, in turn, murdered.

8. To the Samaritans in chapter 8, Philip as well as Peter and John preached Christ; as a result, the demon-possessed were delivered, the lame and paralyzed were healed, and believers received the Holy Spirit.

9. To the government leader from Ethiopia in chapter 8, Philip preached Jesus. After baptizing him in water, Philip was airlifted by the Spirit to Azotus and preached in many more cities.

10. To the Jews in the Damascus synagogues in chapter 9, the newly converted Saul preached that Jesus Christ is the Son of God.

11. To the people of Lydda and Sharon in chapter 9, the sight of a long-term paralytic named Aeneas now healed and walking as a result of Peter praying in the name of Jesus resulted in multitudes turning to Jesus.

12. To the nonbelievers in Joppa, news of the resurrection of a believer (Dorcas) as a result of Peter's prayer caused many to believe in the Lord.

13. To Cornelius, his relatives and friends in chapter 10, Peter preached the death and resurrection of Jesus; the entire Gentile gathering which included nonbelievers was baptized in both the Holy Spirit and water on the same day.

14. To the Jews in Phoenicia, Cyprus, and Antioch in chapter 11, the disciples preached the Word, while believers from Cyprus and Cyrene preached the Lord

Jesus to the Gentiles in Antioch, and many turned to the Lord, with more believers added after Barnabas joined them.

15. To the Jews in the synagogues of Cyprus in chapter 13, Barnabas and Saul preached the Word of God.

16. To Elymas the sorcerer in chapter 13, Paul said, "Will you not cease perverting the straight ways of the Lord? (v.10 NKJV). The proconsul heard Paul and believed.

17. To the Jews in the synagogue in Pisidia in chapter 13, Paul brought glad tidings, that God had raised up Jesus.

18. To the angry Jewish crowd in Pisidia in chapter 13, Paul and Barnabas declared that since they were rejecting the Word of God and eternal life, the apostles would go to the Gentiles—many of whom believed.

19. To the Jews and Greeks in the synagogue in Iconium in chapter 14, Paul and Barnabas spoke boldly about the Lord and His grace, many signs and wonders were performed, and a great multitude believed.

20. To the crowd in Lystra who saw a lame man healed in chapter 14, Paul and Barnabas urged that they should turn from useless idols to the living God.

21. To the large audience in Derbe in chapter 14, Paul and Barnabas preached the gospel and made many new disciples.

22. Their next stop in chapter 14 included Perga, where they preached the Word.

23. After they were imprisoned in Philippi for casting out a girl's evil spirit in the name of Jesus in chapter 16, Paul and Silas told the jailer to believe in Jesus; he and his household were soon saved and baptized.

24. To the Jews in the synagogue of Thessalonica in chapter 17, Paul opened the Scripture and explained that Christ had to suffer and rise again; some Jews and a great multitude of Gentiles were converted.

25. To the Jews in the synagogue of Berea in chapter 17, Paul and Silas preached the Word of God. The Jews searched the Scriptures to see if their claims were true, and many Jews and Gentiles were converted.

26. To the Jews and Greeks and philosophers in Athens in chapter 17, Paul preached Jesus and the resurrection, declaring that the one true God will judge the world by Jesus; several converts were added.

27. To the Jews and Greeks in Corinth in chapter 18, Paul testified that Jesus is the Christ. The ruler of the synagogue and his household turned to Jesus, and many Corinthians were converted and baptized.

28. To the Jews in Achaia in chapter 18, Apollos vigorously refuted their teaching publicly, showing from the Scriptures that Jesus is the Christ.

29. To the Jews and Greeks in Ephesus in chapters 18—19, Paul preached and magnified the name of Jesus on numerous occasions over several years, performing miracles; many converts were added.

30. To the mob in Jerusalem in chapter 22, Paul testified of his vision of Jesus of Nazareth on the road to Damascus and how Ananias had led him in the Sinner's Prayer, calling on the name of the Lord.

31. Under arrest in chapters 22—23, Paul had a couple of conversations with the authorities related to his citizenship and measures to ensure his safety.

32. In an attempt to save his life in front of the Jewish Council in chapter 23, Paul highlighted his hope in the resurrection of the dead.

33. To Felix the governor in chapter 24, Paul again referenced his hope in the resurrection. Later, he spoke about faith in Christ, including a lecture about righteousness, self-control, and the judgment to come. This interaction between Paul and Felix will be further unpacked in the paragraphs ahead.

34. To Felix's successor, Festus, in chapter 25, Paul, still under arrest more than two years later, defended himself and appealed for an audience with Caesar.

35. To Festus the governor and King Agrippa in chapter 26, Paul recounted his salvation story and explained that the prophets and Moses had prophesied that Christ would suffer and rise again. King Agrippa told Paul that he was *almost* persuaded to become a Christian.

36. To the soldiers and fellow prisoners on board the ship bound for Rome in chapter 27, Paul had various conversations about the voyage, food and recommendations for survival in the midst of a great storm.

37. On the island of Malta in chapter 28, Paul prayed for several sick people and they were healed.

38. To the Jewish leaders in Rome in chapter 28, Paul testified of the kingdom of God and all about Jesus for a full day.

39. To his visitors in Rome in chapter 28, Paul preached the kingdom of God and confidently taught the Lord Jesus Christ.

### Abundant Evidence

As Jesus had instructed and predicted, the disciples went *everywhere* preaching the gospel and experienced the signs He had said would accompany their efforts. Sometimes it was a sermon, or a sermon series. Sometimes the gospel came in the form of a stern rebuke. Sometimes it was presented via a long conversation.

Sometimes it was incredibly effective. At times, it was downright refused. On more than one occasion, the preachers were assaulted, persecuted, and even killed.

Of course, the condensed list (above) is just that: condensed. In many of those examples, entire sermons were preached, or lengthy conversations took place. These are simply the headlines. But the considerable size of this sample has to catch our attention today. When there are this many positive examples, we might conclude that God wants us to adopt this pattern as normative. You think?

By comparison, Pentecostals hold passionately to the belief that the gifts of the Spirit discussed repeatedly in the New Testament did not cease with the death of the twelve apostles. While other evangelicals agree and disagree on various points of pneumatology, the most articulate advocates today for the continuation of the baptism of the Holy Spirit with accompanying signs such as speaking in tongues base much of their theology on a pattern of three to five examples cited in these same chapters in Acts.

Suffice it to say, if there were ten or twenty or, my goodness, more than three dozen examples of New Testament believers speaking in tongues, accompanied by even more instructions to do so, few evangelical denominations would exclude tongues as a sign of Holy Spirit baptism from their statements of faith! How could they?

Other issues are, of course, debated among denominations, tribes, members of the same church, or even the same Christian household. What "fun" family conversation did you have last Christmas? The role of women in ministry? The eternal security of the believer? Tithing to the local church? Creation in six 24-hour days or in six eras? Race relations in America? Moderate consumption of alcoholic beverages? Tattoos and piercings? Oops, almost forgot: Is the SEC overrated? (Sorry for raising your blood pressure!)

We all know the list is endless. Yet, which of these camps has more than thirty specific examples in the book of Acts alone?

This pattern about conversations with nonbelievers is utterly foundational. When you are a believer and you are in the presence of unbelievers, the NTN directive is abundantly clear: Find every way possible to bring the love and sacrifice of Jesus into your actions and your conversation.

Paul's interaction with the Roman governor Felix is the one example where, at first glance, there might appear to be an exception. Luke provides insight into the exchange when he says the apostle spoke about "righteousness, self-control, and the coming judgment" (Acts 24:25). But upon further review, it isn't exceptional at all. We must first note that Paul was not a free man in this incident; he was under arrest. The very real threat of execution hung over his head. Second, in this exchange, Paul did not initiate the conversation. He was brought to Felix specifically because Felix wanted to hear from Paul about his *faith in Christ*. What do you do when the man who holds your fate in his hands wants you to come and speak?

You go and speak! Paul understandably wanted to stay alive as long as possible, to continue sharing the gospel.

If Paul spoke about morality with Felix, no mention is made of any specific sins. We can't rule out (or rule in), because we don't know what the "righteousness (and) self-control" parts of the conversation involved. We do know Felix represented Rome, and there were certainly many immoral behaviors throughout Roman culture. If Paul felt led to mention a few societal ills, he would have had a buffet of options from which to choose. We also know that Felix personally lacked scruples; Luke says he later pressured Paul to pay him a bribe to be set free.

In addition, it is commonly accepted (though not referenced in Scripture) that Felix was living in adultery. His wife, Drusilla, was present for this lecture. Maybe Felix directly asked Paul what his faith in Christ would say about their marriage arrangement? Maybe not.

Regardless, the gospel was front and center in this conversation. Luke directly says so, first of all. And then, instead of reading that Felix was offended or angry about a morality debate, we see that he was downright afraid. It was probably that part about "the coming judgment" (v. 25). Does it every time!

Unfortunately, there is no indication here that Felix repented. We are left to conclude that, whether or not Felix's individual transgressions surfaced in any way, the gospel of Jesus as Savior and returning King was undoubtedly emphasized.

### Be Careful about Assumptions

We must reasonably assume that countless other words and conversations not recorded in the book of Acts were exchanged between believers and nonbelievers during those years. Even if the disciples did not initiate the conversation, they no doubt responded to questions if and when they were asked about topics other than the heart of the gospel. I would not imagine for a second that Peter or Paul held back counsel or prayer from someone asking about, for example, sexual temptations. But I have no doubt those unrecorded conversations started and ended with Jesus!

For the record, yes, believers are permitted (and encouraged!) to have normal conversations about everyday life without feeling compelled every time to share the entire plan of salvation. We read, in Paul's case, about very practical (non-gospel) conversations while he was under arrest. With the skill of a defense attorney, he successfully avoided an impending death sentence under hostile circumstances—no small task, considering he was in front of the same group responsible for the murders of Jesus and Stephen! Paul also gave helpful counsel to his pagan guards about surviving the shipwreck, as mentioned above.

But we must also be careful not to assume too much, especially if we are tempted to transfer our assumptions into bedrock support for behaviors we are fond of—such as using God's Word or the name of Jesus to reprimand people about their individual moral or political hang-ups. I don't think I'm alone as a Christ-follower when I cringe at nonbelievers making assumptions about God or the Bible that they feel are logical, but which are out of context.

Some will say, for example, "If Jesus didn't approve of homosexuality and if it's such a big deal, then why isn't there at least one statement attributed to Jesus specifically condemning same-sex relationships?" They make assumptions based on their personal preferences. It is actually true that Jesus did not speak negatively of gay romance during His earthly ministry, as far as we know. But the conclusion that He is okay with that kind of sex is faulty. Jesus specifically affirmed the continuation of the Old Testament view of marriage: a covenant between a man and a woman (see Matthew 19). Even though believers don't read of Him specifically denouncing sexual contact with children or animals, for example, we confidently conclude He opposes any sex outside of marriage in the eyes of God.

It is one thing, therefore, to assume what could have been said or done by the disciples when the cameras weren't rolling, so to speak. It is another matter altogether when we read repeated accounts of what they did, and are then able to directly connect their actions with repeated instructions from Christ. It remains undisputed that the pattern of gospel prioritization when nonbelievers were present was on full display throughout the book of Acts.

## Wise Counsel

A half century ago, Rev. Billy Graham was already proclaiming this message. Listen to his words from a 1967 broadcast of his radio program, *The Hour of Decision:*

> We are never going to reverse the moral trends without a spiritual awakening, and we are never going to have a spiritual awakening until the cross of Jesus Christ is central in all our teaching and preaching.
>
> David Brainerd, in his journal of his life and doings among the American Indians, said, "I never got away from

Jesus and Him crucified. And I found that when my people were gripped by this great evangelical doctrine of Christ and Him crucified, I had no need to give them instructions about morality. I found that one followed as the sure and inevitable fruit of the other."

Dorothy Sayers said, "We have been trying for several centuries to uphold a particular standard of ethical values which derives from Christian dogma, while gradually dispensing with the very dogma which is the sole foundation for those values. If we want Christian behavior, then we must realize that Christian behavior is rooted in Christian belief."

James Stewart, professor of New College in Edinburgh, said, "The driving force of the early Christian mission was not propaganda of beautiful ideals of the brotherhood of man; it was proclamation of the mighty acts of God. ... At the very heart of the apostles' message stood the divine redemptive deed on Calvary."

If the church wants high, moral standards in the nation and a new social justice, then let the church get back to preaching the simple, authoritative gospel of Jesus Christ in the power of the Holy Spirit.

It was this gospel that brought about many of the great social reforms of the past. The preaching of the cross and the resurrection have been primarily responsible for promoting humanitarian sentiment and social concern during the last 400 years. Prison reform, the prohibition of the slave trade, the abolition of slavery, improvement in working conditions, the protection of children, the crusade against cruelty to animals are the outcomes of great religious awakenings brought about by the proclamation of the gospel.

Dr. F. L. Foakes-Jackson, the distinguished church historian, said, "History shows that the thought of Christ on the cross has been more potent than anything else in arousing a compassion for suffering and indignation at injustice."

But what are we witnessing today? Many of our ecclesiastical organizations are making resolutions and pronouncements. They are lobbying to bring into being and enforce the social changes envisioned by church leaders as a part of the world where the church shall be the dominating influence. When most major Protestant denominations have their annual councils, assemblies or conventions, they make pronouncements on matters having to do with disarmament, federal aid to education, birth control, the United Nations, and any number of social and political issues.

The changing of lives is a primary mission of the church. The only way to change people is to get them converted to Jesus Christ. Then they will have the capacity to live up to the Christian command to "love thy neighbor" (Matthew 22:39).[32]

It refreshes me to hear that powerful admonition from a man who knows what he's talking about. But this is not outdated philosophy. This, thankfully, is present reality in many churches and missions organizations.

## The Gospel Does Its Work

Every pastor I know from Africa reinforces this truth. I've had the pleasure of meeting Barnabas Mtokambali who serves as the spiritual leader ("superintendent") for a Pentecostal organization in Tanzania. This nation, on Africa's eastern coast, is one of many regions where the church is growing rapidly. Under his leadership, the Assemblies of God launched a ten-year "Tanzania for Jesus" campaign in 2008 with an aggressive plan aimed at planting thousands of new churches, training thousands of new pastors, building multiple church planting schools, training scores of new believers, and sending missionary families to other countries.

How has it gone? Since the launch of this campaign less than ten years ago, they have established about 50 permanent church planting schools and started thousands of new congregations, bringing their total to over 7,500 churches. And they're not finished yet! I had the privilege of witnessing the church's efforts during a visit in 2017.

Their focus is squarely on presenting the gospel to unbelievers. Their leaders regularly emphasize the importance of gospel prioritization when training ministers and church leaders. In their church planting schools, the pastors are taught to become fishermen. They win people to Jesus first, then "clean them up" afterward.

While sex outside of marriage is an epidemic in Western cultures, a prevalent challenge in parts of Africa is men having too many wives at the same time. Polygamy is legal in the majority of African nations. Conversely, it is illegal across North America. However, when it comes to homosexuality, the legal status is nearly reversed for both continents. Just as homosexuality is a prevalent concern of many Western churches, polygamy is a constant challenge in much of Africa.

Barnabas relates the story of a recent convert in Tanzania. A man with four wives and many children was deathly ill. He sought the help of local witch doctors, but did not get any better. Desperate for healing, he also consulted with Muslim and Hindu spiritual leaders. As a last resort, he attended an evangelistic crusade, where he heard about Jesus.

Upon hearing the call to repent and turn to Jesus, he surrendered his heart to Christ and received prayer for physical healing as well. To the delight of this man and his whole family, he was divinely healed in body, mind and spirit.

As he began attending church regularly and learning God's Word, he concluded after some time that having four wives was inconsistent with biblical teaching. In a sobering conversation, he told his wives he did not feel he could remain married to multiple partners and expect God's favor to remain on his life. How do you solve a problem like this?

Barnabas laughed as he told me that all of his wives concurred. With the help of their local church leadership, they worked out a plan for him to remain married to only one of the women. At the same time, he continues financial support for the other three women and the children they had with him. Salvation has come to his entire household! The focus that made this possible was preaching about Jesus, not "Polygamy is wrong. Polygamists are going to hell."

This illustrates a powerful directive found throughout the New Testament. Jesus Himself prepared His disciples, and us, with the proper mindset about prioritizing the gospel with nonbelievers, instead of individual sinful behaviors. He said,

"Nevertheless I tell you the truth. It is to your advantage that I go away; for if I do not go away, the Helper will not come to you; but if I depart, I will send Him to you. And when He has come, He will convict the world of sin, and of righteousness, and of judgment: *of sin, because they do not believe in Me*; of righteousness, because I go to My Father and you see Me no more; of judgment, because the ruler of this world is judged" (John 16:7-11 NKJV).

Memorize this! Let it marinate in your soul: What is this world's sin that has the focus of the Holy Spirit? *Not believing in Jesus!* Doesn't it always feel safest to follow the leading of the Spirit? If we want to challenge nonbelievers about their sin, can we agree that the Holy Spirit's way is best?

If so, let's invest our passion for confrontation where it belongs. Let's challenge the world to repent and believe in Jesus, to join us in heaven, instead of wasting our energies (and theirs) challenging heathens to see our way on sex, drugs, and rock 'n' roll.

The apostle Peter piles on with his admonition to focus on the gospel as the antidote for the variety of misbehaviors among nonbelievers: "For we have spent enough of our past lifetime in doing the will of the Gentiles—when we walked in lewdness, lusts, drunkenness, revelries, drinking parties, and abominable idolatries. In regard to these, they think it strange that you do not run with them in the same flood of dissipation, speaking evil of you. They will give an account to Him who is ready to judge the living and the dead. For this reason the gospel was preached also to those who are dead, that they might be judged according to men in the flesh, but live according to God in the spirit" (1 Peter 4:3-6 NKJV).

Our righteous behavior will seem strange to nonbelieving perverts, partiers, and drunks. They might even speak evil of us. When they begin to pressure us to adopt their sinful lifestyles, what should we do? Criticize their moral choices? Get involved with their sin?

No! Preach the gospel so they can live!

## Becoming Doers of the Word

In light of this substantial pattern of instruction and experience, Bible believers have to ask themselves if this is some colossal coincidence, or if there really is something God wants His children to grasp and then put into practice.

Another way of saying it is: *If we want to make a case for debates with nonbelievers about anything other than the gospel of the kingdom, we'll have to base our approach on something other than the examples of the apostles and disciples, or the teachings of Christ for that matter.*

Gulp.

# GET THE MESSAGE?

The Great Commission given by the risen Christ to His apostles included an intentional sequence: preach the gospel, baptize converts, then teach them how to follow Christ.

In more than three dozen specific conversations with nonbelievers in the book of Acts, there is not a single example of the disciples harping on immorality or politics; their focus and their zeal never wavered from the gospel.

Fifty years ago, Dr. Billy Graham declared, "The only way to change people is to get them converted to Jesus Christ. Then they will have the capacity to live up to the Christian command to 'love thy neighbor.'"

According to Jesus Himself, the Holy Spirit's concern in convicting the world of sin is focused on their refusal to believe in Jesus.

# WDJD? WHAT *DID* JESUS DO?

Up until this point, most of our examples have purposefully centered on the apostles, following Pentecost. But what about Jesus Himself? What do the four Gospels reveal?

After all, it's one thing to observe that Christ-followers such as Paul and Peter never confronted believers in front of the world. And neither did they forsake the gospel to debate morality with nonbelievers. But, one might argue, they were merely imperfect followers, doing what they could just to get by from day to day.

Jesus, on the other hand, could see the future. Knowing that believers then and now would all look to Him for positive patterns, what clues did He leave us? Did Jesus, our prime example, make a habit of chastising nonbelievers about their lifestyles? When He was talking to nonbelievers, did He throw fellow believers under the bus, or not? In this chapter, we will take an in-depth look into the interactions of Jesus with Gentiles.

Before we cite specific examples, we need to briefly revisit a point from the previous chapter. As was mentioned, there was a substantial change in definition between the accounts of the Gospels and the accounts of the Epistles. In the centuries, years, and even days leading up to the crucifixion, God's people were mainly believing Jews (along with relatively few Gentiles who converted), headed for the same heaven as you and me. Specifically, Jews who devoutly loved and worshiped God and kept the commandments of the Law, including having proper sacrifices offered by the priests for their sins.

Even up until the crucifixion, we can rightly assume that Jews who followed Jesus, including the disciples, continued to participate in Old Testament sacrifices. Mark 1 records that Jesus healed a leper and then sent him to the priest for offering the sacrifices prescribed by Moses. Prior to Christ's suffering and resurrection, there was no other atoning sacrifice.

Then the cross ushered in a pivotal transformation—not only among the Jews but among the Gentiles, too. The whole purpose of Christ's sacrifice and resurrection was to drastically alter the membership requirements of heaven. A life of grace and faith-driven obedience became the powerful and effective replacement for the requirements of law and animal sacrifices. In Acts and the Epistles, we see a purposeful shift in the identity of God's people.

Consequently, the defining marks of God's children prior to Calvary—who they are, and aren't—is unquestionably different from their makeup after. For starters, before the atonement, there isn't even any reference in Scripture to "believers." This term is not used until Acts. The quickest parallel term used in the prior time period of the Gospels would be "worshipers."

This may seem like splitting hairs. Don't worshipers believe? Absolutely. Can you be a true believer without worshiping?

Absolutely not. Point made. But the distinction is helpful for this important conversation.

Thus, in the eyes of some, "believers vs. nonbelievers" in Acts and the Epistles would be roughly equivalent to "worshipful and Law-abiding Jews vs. disobedient Jews" in the Gospels. Or, "worshipful, Law-abiding Jews vs. pretty much all Gentiles," unless the Gentile(s) had converted to worshiping the God of the Jews. Jesus' ministry among worshipful Jews ("devout" is another valid label) had clear parallels for the apostles' ministry among believers.

A more simplified and traditional understanding, of course, would be that all Jews were God's people; they were just exhibiting varying degrees of worshipful obedience or sinful disobedience. Due to their heritage, all Jews would then be considered believers by birth who, as adults, were either complying with God's laws or rebelling against them. For the sake of this chapter's conversation, I will proceed with this understanding.

## Did He Practice What He Prescribed?

Let's continue, then, by revisiting Christ's Matthew 18 admonition to confront fellow believers privately, inside the community of worshipers. Any casual student of the Gospels readily acknowledges that Jesus was no stranger to confrontation.

But did He follow His own Matthew 18 counsel? Or did He occasionally ridicule believers (worshipers) in the company of nonbelievers? Specifically, did Jesus challenge or bash Jews for their sins and offenses when unconverted Gentiles were watching? If not Jesus, did His associates? Have you ever thought about that? I readily confess that I never paid any attention to that line of thinking until now.

Unquestionably, major facets of Jesus' earthly life and ministry will never be replicated. He was the only Messiah, for example, and many of His actions and encounters, such as His substitutionary work on the cross, were understandably meant to stand alone. Likewise, His contemporaries such as His disciples and John the Baptist responded to numerous once-in-forever circumstances. Still, much of what we read about the actions of Christ in the Gospels purposefully serves as the model for all His disciples, then and throughout the ages. "Follow me as I follow Christ," Paul affirmed (1 Corinthians 11:1).

Jesus challenged and stretched His disciples on numerous occasions. Consistent with His own teachings, Jesus directly confronted Peter, James, and John, for example, more than once. It is safe to refer to these individuals as devout Jews. Though imperfect, they were worshipful of God, obedient to the Law, and had placed their faith in Jesus as Messiah.

When Jesus called them out, it was not always for blatant sins. Often, it was for their misunderstanding of kingdom principles—for example, "Get behind me, Satan!" (Mark 8:33). "You do not know what you are asking" (Matt. 20:22). Jesus made a clear habit of giving course correction to those closest to Him.

One abrupt and necessary confrontation of a disciple happened in the garden as Jesus was being arrested by the crowd of priests and temple guards, led by Judas the betrayer. With an impassioned effort certifiably unique to that moment in history, Peter used his sword in an attempt to protect the Messiah from arrest and execution, injuring the high priest's servant in the process. Jesus prohibited further harm to Peter and everyone else by confronting him in front of all those Jews; (John's Gospel indicates the presence of Roman soldiers, too). "Put your sword back in its place" (Matt. 26:52). Further, Jesus healed the servant's ear, which apparently spared Peter from being instantly attacked or arrested. This wasn't about a prior personal offense against Jesus; it was happening in real time to someone else. And, it was no doubt viewed by the authorities as an illegal, criminal offense. All exceptions to Matthew 18, as we noted in chapter 3.

Regardless, in no case do we see Jesus dragging up the previous sinful offenses of His disciples in front of nonbelievers or speaking negatively about them behind their back. He always confronted them *directly*.

And Jesus dealt with many more Jews than His twelve disciples. John's Gospel records several examples of "sin no more" admonitions given by Jesus to several Jews: for example, the lame man at the Pool of Bethesda in chapter 5, also the woman caught in adultery in chapter 8. In both stories, each received incredible help from Jesus first. The lame man was healed, and the woman's life was spared from stoning by the Jewish leaders. There is nothing that leads us to believe that either individual was anything but Jewish, bound by birth to uphold the law.

Most conclude these encounters led both Jews to believe in Jesus as Lord. In both cases, Jesus confronted them about their sin discreetly, *after* He met their need, and without any evidence of anger. And notice that Jesus gave the woman His admonition *privately* to sin no more, after her Jewish accusers had all slunk away (John 8:9).

## On the Other Hand

There was, however, a special category of Jews who were part of the hypocritical religious structure of the day. Jesus, and even John the Baptist, confronted these leaders publicly on numerous occasions. From the top down, these included King Herod (Antipas), the chief priests, the scribes and Pharisees, the Sadducees, and the moneychangers in the temple.

On the one hand, many Jews (and Gentiles) would have perceived all of these to be practicing Jews ("worshipers") due to their roles. They were supposedly leaders of God's people, though they all operated under varying degrees of license and authority from Rome. On the other hand, we get the clear impression from the Gospels that most lacked purity in their worship. They of course claimed to be on God's side, followers of the Law, on their way to heaven. But Jesus repeatedly highlighted the complete corruption of their internal motivations, rendering their outward obedience moot for kingdom purposes.

Jesus' death at Calvary would not only put them out of business in God's eyes, it completely changed the salvation paradigm. On those grounds alone, it is fair to say this group warrants unique classification in terms of Christian history, both past and present. It is rather interesting to observe how this dying breed of seemingly religious people were treated, especially when they were confronted for wrongdoing.

Compelling arguments could be made that most of these Jewish leaders were already outside God's true family before Jesus even "hit the ground." If so, then Christ's multiple rebukes would not be comparable for confronting fellow believers. For this discussion, however, we continue to employ the approach that all of them were viewed as God's people since they were Jews. And, at least a few of them were sincere worshipers. Further, regardless of the condition of their hearts, it is fair to say they were widely regarded by the house of Israel to be legitimate leaders of God's people, which clearly troubled the Messiah. Watch how this assumption, that people perceived them as devout Jewish worshipers, was consistently played out in the many examples we see in the interactions they had with Jesus.

One of the most well-known confrontations is the episode of Jesus' demonstrative rebuke in the Jerusalem temple. All four Gospel writers tell how Jesus overturned the moneychangers' tables. In fact, it appears Jesus may have done this on two different occasions.

Matthew, Mark, and Luke seem to be describing the same event, near the end of Christ's earthly ministry. All three of them say Jesus quoted from Isaiah, accusing the moneychangers of turning God's "house of prayer" into a "den of thieves." They were profiteering from sincere people who simply wanted to give offerings to God as an act of worship.

John's account, on the other hand, appears toward the start of Jesus' ministry. John uniquely cites Jesus referring to "my Father's house" being turned into "a house of merchandise." Further, John makes it clear that Jesus' actions and demeanor were impassioned, citing His use of a whip of cords to clear out the offenders, along with their livestock. His intensity reminded the disciples of the time that King David said he was "consumed" by zeal for God's house (Ps. 69:9).

In both exchanges, we find Jesus confronting Jews directly. He was, after all, in the temple, where Jewish leaders and followers assembled regularly to hear the Scripture, to pray, and to have the priests offer sacrifices for their sins. Gentiles were nearby too; they weren't forbidden to enter the temple's outer courts, which is where the moneychangers set up shop.

Jesus confronted Jews who were actively corrupting the temple right in front of Him, tainting the process of holy redemption, in direct disobedience to Old Testament provisions. Jesus confronted them directly. Nothing about this rebuke compromised what He prescribed in Matthew 18.

Why do I highlight this particular incident? Because it is often cited as the basis for today's Christians to take a stand on moral issues. "If Jesus drove out the moneychangers, Christians shouldn't back down either."

In context, that claim has some validity. If people are distorting the provisions of salvation, passionate confrontation is needed at times, especially if their twisting of the gospel is on full display, as it was in this case. This is true whether those perverting the gospel are believers or not.

But I would offer two notable clarifications. First, this was the Jewish Messiah directly confronting Jews. They were strongly rebuked because they were God's people perverting God's holy process for redemption—not because they were nonbelievers struggling with booze, recreational marijuana, or a progressive social cause.

Similarly, Elymas the Jewish false prophet and sorcerer was aggressively confronted by Paul in Acts 13 for frustrating the work of the gospel. Heaven got in on that act and caused Elymas to become blind. Directly distorting and frustrating the message of salvation merits confrontation, even passionate confrontation when appropriate.

Second, any fair reading of the four Gospels shows us that angry rebuking was hardly the norm for Jesus. Rather, it was unquestionably the exception. Valid, for sure, but rare. Instead, what we see as normal confrontation by Jesus was to give calm but firm rebuke when appropriate, often after meeting the person's physical or spiritual need first. In no case, even in the temple with the moneychangers, did Jesus approach a level of anger or passion that was out of control. His emotions were always subject to Him, never the other way around. The same should be true of every Christ-follower.

The Jews who received by far the lion's share of rebuke from Jesus were the hypocritical Jewish leaders: priests and scribes, Pharisees and Sadducees. All four Gospels record repeated examples of Jesus attempting to set them straight. He even critiqued them publicly when He taught, citing them as examples of what not to do. Frankly, with the sheer abundance of these rebukes found in Scripture, I was admittedly stunned when I discovered that Matthew 18 was never violated, even in these numerous accounts.

Reading all four Gospels in chronological context, we see that Jesus confronted these leaders directly on several occasions *before* He began to castigate them in front of other Jews. As was the case with Paul, it is not only okay but necessary to publicly call out those who identify as believers but who refuse to turn from their sin after repeated warnings.

Regardless of the individual heart conditions, we don't see Jesus calling out these perceived leaders of the Jewish faith in front of Gentiles. An interesting example is found with a trail of events beginning in the story found in Matthew 8, Mark 5, and Luke 8, where Jesus is ministering in a Gentile community.

All three Gospels tell how Jesus delivered a Gentile man who was possessed by demons. He is described as being from the region of the Gadarenes. After he was delivered, he traveled the ten cities of the Decapolis (all Gentile locations) and spread the news of Jesus and His miracle-working power.

Later, in Matthew 14 and Mark 6, we see Jesus and His disciples returning to this area, where multitudes of people now recognized Him, thanks to the former demoniac's testimony. Every sick Gentile touched by Jesus on this return visit was healed.

Then, in Matthew 15 and Mark 7, the Pharisees and scribes who had traveled all the way from Jerusalem to this Gentile region began to confront Jesus. They were troubled that His disciples were not washing their hands before they ate bread. Jesus responded directly with a confrontation of His own, and it was a sharp rebuke.

In both Matthew and Mark, interesting updates on the audience are then provided. The Gentile crowds were not around when the direct confrontation with the scribes and Pharisees took place. Only *after* that frank interchange does the Scripture proceed to say, "He called the crowds and said to them …" (Matt. 15:10).

It seems clear that Jesus was aware that the false concerns raised by the Pharisees about hand-washing may have been circulating. Without mentioning Jewish leaders in a negative fashion in the hearing of so many Gentiles as He did on other occasions with Jewish audiences, Jesus taught a spiritual lesson to the Gentiles present (along with some Jews, no doubt). He made it clear that we are not defiled by what is on the outside coming in (hands covered in dirt). Rather, the problem lies with what is on the inside of us coming out (the spiritual infection of our hearts). Jesus used the opportunity to focus on the heart of the gospel (our hearts need to be forgiven) and avoided direct ridicule or mention of Jewish leaders in the process.

Later, when the crowds had gone, and only Jews (His disciples) remained, Jesus resumed more direct speaking with candor about the Jewish leaders—that is, if you think calling the Pharisees "blind leaders of the blind" might be a less-than-flattering indictment. But we can cite no such derogatory statements made of Jewish religious leaders by Jesus with Gentiles present.

I am floored. Why are the details of that account so painstakingly provided for us? The timing. The audience. The words spoken. The discipline demonstrated. By two different Gospel writers. I am convinced that this was not by accident. It paints a visible reinforcement of Jesus' repeated teachings and example: *Stay on script. Focus on the gospel. Don't speak ill of brothers and sisters in front of nonbelievers, even when they aren't behaving like brothers and sisters.*

There is, however, one undeniable case where Jesus said something derogatory about Jewish religious leaders in front of a Gentile. Under arrest, facing crucifixion, and responding to repeated lies about His identity, Jesus chastised the chief priests, specifically Caiaphas the high priest, in front of Pilate,

> **Don't speak ill of brothers and sisters in front of nonbelievers, even when they aren't behaving like brothers and sisters.**

the Roman governor. Jesus told Pilate that His accuser had "the greater sin." Pilate was, of course, 100 percent Gentile.

This was clearly at the end of Jesus' earthly ministry, long after His instruction in Matthew 18.

For years, He had repeatedly confronted the priests, directly and with numerous witnesses. Caiaphas, the high priest, and his cohorts were the chief prosecutors against the Messiah. As such, those religious leaders in particular were clearly outside of the family of God at this point.

So, in perfect alignment with Matthew 18, Jesus was treating them exactly as He instructed us to do. Under arrest, Jesus complied with the request of a Gentile holding earthly authority over Him, Pilate, telling him the truth about others whom Jesus and His followers now justifiably viewed like heathens and tax collectors.

## Hard-hitting John

How about those who were on Jesus' team? John the Baptist, not exactly known as a wallflower, challenged more than a few Jews. When asked for spiritual advice by tax collectors and soldiers in Luke 3, he didn't hold back. He told the tax collectors to be honest, only collecting what was actually due. Then he advised the soldiers to do no violence toward anyone and to avoid bearing false witness. He also told them to be content with their wages. On the surface, his comments appear to fall within the bounds of moral teaching.

But what if it is somehow argued that he was rebuking them for specific wrongs they had done, even though they specifically asked him to speak into their lives? After all, he had just preached to the whole crowd about repentance.

Tax collectors, like Matthew and Zaccheus before they followed Jesus, were so despised because they were Jews who made the lives of their Jewish brothers and sisters miserable, all in the name of Rome. And many commentators conclude these were likely Jewish soldiers of Herod the tetrarch. Though tax collectors and soldiers all operated under the ultimate authority of Rome, there is no indication that Gentiles were present in this crowd full of people claiming Abraham was their father. Plus, they all came to John to be baptized in water. Though John's unique call to baptism was heaven-sent, ceremonial washings (baptisms) were Jewish in their origins (Leviticus 16, for example).

John the Baptist also confronted Herod, accusing him of breaking the law by marrying his sister-in-law Herodias. While the generations of Herods were originally of Arab and not Jewish descent, they identified as Jews, practicing numerous components of their religion. John was confronting someone who claimed his position as a leader of the Jews, God's people. As such, he was clearly expected to uphold Jewish law, and when he married Herodias, he broke that law. Apparently, he did many other unlawful or immoral things that John felt free to rebuke.

This is an appropriate point to hit the "pause button" on the discussion of Jews being confronted. It cannot be overlooked that John the Baptist's repudiation of Herod's adultery did not produce the desired effect. Like Felix the governor, whom we discussed in the previous chapter (and whom some speculate Paul might have confronted about his adultery), Herod showed no signs of repenting of adultery either. Most tragically, both adulterous politicians failed to follow Jesus Christ as Savior.

Although we are referring to Herod here as a Jew, how could either of these adultery confrontations possibly lend support to the notion that chastising nonbelievers for their immorality is God's preferred approach? Really chew on this: How many examples does the New Testament provide where nonbelievers were clearly rebuked for their immoral acts and then had a change of heart? None.

What then *is* the cure for adultery? Make no mistake, the New Testament is full of examples of nonbelieving adulterers who *did* abandon and overcome their immorality. Paul spells out the remedy very clearly: Jesus! Adulterers—along with thieves, drunks, extortioners, and homosexuals—are washed, sanctified, and justified "in the name of the Lord Jesus by the Spirit of our God" (1 Corinthians 6:11). And how would he know? "Such were *some of you*," he said in the same breath. Remember, these are the same immoral heathens with whom Paul began his relationship by *preaching Christ and Him crucified,* not by harping on their immoral habits.

Returning now to John the Baptist, the key is to grasp that he was the last in a very long line of the pre-Calvary prophets. On the one hand, the correction that John provided before his execution can be seen as a Jewish prophet doing what Jewish prophets did before Calvary. In large part, they taught and corrected Jews, including Jewish leaders, who should know better. But John's confrontation justifiably had a unique sense of imminent hope and urgency. *Get ready, Jews! Your Messiah is almost here. The kingdom of God is at hand; now is the time to repent and get your house in order.*

Thus, this is by no means an apples-to-apples basis for believers today seeking to frame John's approach as a biblical justification for chastising nonbelievers about their immorality. Funny how we sometimes extract and misapply that part of John's behavior as exemplary without feeling one bit compelled to don camel hair or dine on locusts. (There's *eating clean*, and then there's *eating gross*.)

Instead, John's pattern is consistent with what we see throughout the entire New Testament; God's people rebuke God's people for their spiritual misbehavior at times, but not in front of pagans. Jesus consistently modeled and taught this approach, and the disciples simply picked up where He left off. On what possible biblical basis could any Christian leader today conclude it is permissible to make a habit of critiquing fellow believers with nonbelievers watching and listening? Especially if no conscientious efforts to work out differences privately have been attempted first!

## What about Gentiles?

Next, are there any patterns, or even single examples, of Jesus confronting Gentiles about their sinful lifestyles? Not that I can find.

During the time of Jesus' public ministry, soldiers and leaders from Rome kept a constant if uneasy eye on Jewish territories. Gentiles traveled throughout Judea. Samaritans were there, too, but they were not considered Gentiles even though they were clearly not Jews. Due to their mixed heritage, they were half-breeds. In the eyes of many Jews, Samaritans were in fact more despised than Gentiles.

So Jesus had plenty of opportunities to challenge nonbelieving or nonconverted Gentiles and Samaritans about their morality. For example, Gentiles were likely in the crowd when Jesus preached His most famous sermon; Matthew 4:25 notes that the multitudes following Jesus included people from Decapolis. This was a region heavily populated by Gentiles.

But the entire Sermon on the Mount appears directed at followers of Jesus, regardless if they were Jews or converted Gentiles. Why is that a safe assumption? Jesus would not have told nonbelievers that they were the "salt of the earth" or the "light of the world." Neither would pagan Gentiles have been expected to appreciate His references to Old Testament law that He was now endorsing in the sermon and expanding to the heart level.

And, ultimately, there is no direct challenge to a nonbeliever contained in this account. From start to finish, this masterpiece has the marks of a sermon intended for God's people, specifically those who are already following Christ, whether Jew or Gentile. The entire sermon concludes with the Jewish-oriented crowd appreciating the contrast in teaching style between Jesus and "their teachers of the law" (Matt. 7:29 NIV).

Note: The fact that the crowd was full of God-worshipers and not pagans gives further legitimacy to the less-than-flattering reference to the scribes and Pharisees offered during the sermon. Although this account comes early in Matthew, the Luke presentation comes not until chapter 6, after Jesus had directly challenged the Jewish leaders more than a few times. In other words, this is not a case of Jesus airing the dirty laundry of fellow believers before giving them multiple chances to reconcile. To the contrary!

Jesus also had one-on-one encounters with numerous individuals who weren't Jewish. The Roman centurion in Matthew 8 and the Syrophoenician woman in Matthew 15 are two such cases. Both of their respective cultures embraced numerous immoral practices. But we don't hear Jesus lecturing either of them about morality in any way. The interaction centered instead around His role as Messiah and Healer. Maybe that has something to do with why both of them were drawn to Christ.

Luke records at least two episodes related to Samaritans. In chapter 9, he tells us that an entire Samaritan village rejected Jesus, refusing to receive His teaching. When James and John proposed calling down fire from heaven to consume the village, Jesus rebuked His disciples while refusing to condemn the Samaritans. "The Son of Man did not come to destroy men's lives but to save them," He said (Luke 9:56).

Then, in chapter 17, we read of a Samaritan leper who was healed by Jesus. He was the only one out of ten lepers healed who returned to thank Jesus. But neither story references Jesus addressing their immorality.

John captured the famous story of the Samaritan woman at the well. She became an avid promoter of Jesus as the Messiah after having a life-changing conversation with Him. We later see that many in her village turned to Christ as a result of her powerful testimony.

This encounter is sometimes mischaracterized as something other than what it was. There is no record of Jesus condemning her for her many marriages. He didn't tell her, as He did others, to "go and sin no more." In fact, He gave her a backhanded compliment about her honesty before supernaturally "reading her mail." Through divine inspiration, Jesus knew full well that she had had five previous husbands and was now with yet another man. Her response, then, to His request for her to go and bring her husband was a softball for Jesus to hit out of the park.

When she retorted that she had no husband, Jesus had the open door to reveal Himself as Messiah. He responded by telling her something that would unquestionably signal His divine origin. When she heard Him absolutely nail her marital history without ever having met her before, she replied, "I perceive that you are a prophet." She knew He was no normal Jew, or human being for that matter.

His powerful revelation, somewhat resembling a "word of knowledge" described in 1 Corinthians 12, was void of any condemnation or debates about adultery. None. The focus was the gospel. "I who speak to you am He" (the Messiah—John 4:26). And she believed Him with her whole heart. She wasn't chastised for immorality; she was introduced to the Savior of the world!

And her actions demonstrated that was the case. She immediately ran through her whole village telling people about what happened. Did she invite them to come meet a man who told her adultery was wrong? No, her emphasis was on Jesus' divinity. "Come, see a Man who told me all things that I ever did. Could this be the Christ?" (John 4:29). It worked, because many in her village believed in Jesus.

Granted, telling a single woman that she is currently cohabitating, and that she has had five previous husbands, can sound an awful lot like confronting a nonbeliever about their immoral lifestyle. But the manner in which Jesus started the conversation about His living water, followed by His masterful set-up of the seeming curiosity about her marriage history, appears incredibly intentional. The entire exchange was focused on revealing Himself as the Christ, not rebuking a marginalized woman.

This was jaw-dropping divine revelation! Unlike many modern conversations where believers chastise nonbelievers for their well-known immoral activities, the knowledge of this woman's background was supernaturally achieved. Such revelation, then and now, unquestionably spotlights the authentic divinity of God. It makes one wonder. Any believers somehow seeking to cite this particular episode as the basis for challenging a nonbelievers' immorality must certainly feel obliged to gain the knowledge of the misbehavior strictly through divine channels, right?

It should not shock or surprise us today that God still has priorities in His messaging. During the ministry of Jesus and all the early church leaders we read about, the priority is on proclaiming the gospel to nonbelievers. Judging and confrontation about morality are reserved for post-salvation preaching and conversations.

> **Did you catch that? The person with the speck in the eye is our brother (or sister)—not someone who doesn't yet know what it's like to be set free in Jesus.**

In demonstrating the pattern of instruction and experience related to nonbelievers in our audience, the apostles were simply continuing the thorough example set by Jesus.

As a final illustration, consider this. Without ambiguity, Jesus directly cautions us against hypocritically calling out the sins of others: "First remove the plank that is in your own eye, and then you will see clearly to remove the speck that is in your brother's eye" (Luke 6:42 NKJV).

Did you catch that? The person with the speck is our *brother (or sister)*—not someone who doesn't yet know what it's like to be set free in Jesus. This word picture caps Jesus' prohibition against judging hypocritically. When Jesus said, "Judge not," He was warning a crowd of *believers* about the potential for improper attitudes toward their *fellow believers.*

In his 2016 sermon series "Twisted," Craig Groeschel, pastor of Life.Church, explained and expounded the judging concept this way:

We never hold non-Christians to Christian standards. We never hold those who are outside the family of God to our own family standards.

In fact, this is what Paul said in 1 Corinthians 5:12: "What business is it of mine to judge those outside the church?" If they're not Jesus-followers, who am I to tell them they should be living any different way? That's none of my business. Then he (Paul) says, "Are you not to judge those inside? It's God's to judge those outside."

If they are believers, aren't we together as iron sharpens iron supposed to help one another, spur one another on toward good works, to show love, to help gently restore people who've fallen away? Aren't we to help other family members? At my house, we have certain rules, or certain shows we don't watch. Certain language we don't use. I can't hold your kids accountable for my family rules. Not my business. (That's) your family.

If someone is outside the family of God, we don't hold them accountable to Christian family rules. It's not our place to judge. This is probably the number one reason why so many non-Christians step away from ever pursuing God because (of) the judgmentalism and hypocrisy of Christian believers.[33]

The apostles, then, were simply following the approach they had already observed in Jesus when nonbelievers were watching. Jesus provided a strong and memorable pattern of both instruction and experience that they would need to draw on repeatedly in the months and years after His ascension.

It nudges us to ask ourselves: Why get tripped up on confusing communication that frustrates Kingdom advances when we can choose a far more effective message?

# GET THE
# MESSAGE?

Even before the accounts of Acts and the rest of the New Testament, the Gospels laid a strong foundation for considering our audience of nonbelievers by demonstrating how Christ and His contemporaries handled similar conversations.

Not surprisingly, Jesus never violated His own instruction about believers reconciling prior sinful offenses in stages, inside the church.

Two adulterers in the Gospels were rebuked for their immorality: Herod (by John the Baptist) and the woman caught in adultery (by Jesus). Both were lawbreaking Jews, not unbelieving pagans.

In the numerous accounts of Jesus amongst Gentile nonbelievers, we never see Him rebuking them for their immorality or politics nor can we cite any examples of Him speaking negatively in front of nonbelievers about those who worshiped God.

# 9

# AN EXCEPTIONAL GOSPEL

I have a running joke with a good buddy in his early fifties with whom I share the same birthday. Due to what I insist on calling his *advanced age*, he mysteriously has a hard time remembering that he is exactly one year older than I am. Of course, I dutifully remind him every year on his birthday.

As fellow ministers, we worked in the same office years ago and attended numerous events together. Consequently, we heard many of the same speakers and the same messages. With relative frequency, one particular illustration would surface in messages we heard. It was the story of the child on the beach who saved one starfish among countless others by throwing it back into the ocean.

We were in mild disbelief whenever audience members responded as though they'd never heard that anecdote before. The original essay was called *The Star Thrower* by Loren Eiseley, written in the late 1960s. Various versions had been told and retold over the years. It made its way onto greeting cards and into numerous sermons.

We'd often shake our heads, sometimes in amazement, as audience members inevitably smiled and even cried upon hearing the punchline right before an impassioned altar call. How could they possibly be hearing this for the first time? Who knows? Maybe we were just bitter preachers, envious that we didn't know how to craft such a good finale.

Decades later, the phenomenon shows no sign of letting up. I heard a valedictorian share it recently at a high school graduation. As if on cue, the entire audience sat on the edge of their seats, spellbound in anticipation of the story's mysterious end. Are you kidding me!

Today, all my buddy has to do in a conversation is utter the words "It mattered to *that* starfish, John." And we both crack up laughing.

## The Greatest Story

There's a much older story that elicits yawns from some people while still fascinating millions. It is *The Greatest Story Ever Told*—the gospel. This priceless, precious story constantly deserves renewed understanding and appreciation by those who know and communicate it. How unfortunate when we who should revere it most become so familiar with its themes that we forget the truly exceptional message.

The sworn enemies of the gospel don't seem to have that problem. In the summer of 2016, ISIS devoted an issue of their propaganda magazine *Dabiq* to this matter. The feature article "Breaking the Cross" alleged that Jesus was never crucified. In calling for all-out warfare against Christians, they did not seem to care too much about distinctions between churches or denominations. If anyone or any group supported the salvation work of the cross, ISIS called for their annihilation unless they converted to Islam.

When the gospel's enemies understand how critical its message is, its followers ought to understand its power even more! There's nothing like the gospel. Period. It expresses the heartbeat of God, how He loves us so much He would permit His only begotten Son to be sacrificed in such a horrible fashion as the cross. It reveals the sole vehicle through which mankind can discover the only means for forgiveness and eternal life. And yet, the gospel is even more powerful and unique than we often imagine.

On the one hand, it is history's most *inclusive* story, in that the gospel means all are welcome at the Father's table. Regardless of past sins, regardless of faith history, regardless of political persuasion, regardless of gender, nationality, race, or age, the gospel invites everyone to enjoy forgiveness and eternal life. But at the same time it is absolutely *exclusive* in terms of being in a league all its own.

Here are five reasons why the gospel is eminently exclusive:

1. Its *Author.* Yes, that seems obvious, but it bears mentioning. No other faith besides Christianity fully reflects the heart of God.
2. Its *content.* The gospel of Jesus Christ presents the one and only means of reconciliation with our heavenly Father.
3. The *conviction of its carriers.* Who else besides sincere followers of Christ espouse the view that all have sinned and that forgiveness and eternal life in heaven are ours through faith in a risen Christ, and Christ alone? With no add-ons. What other group makes that claim?

4. Its *unifying power.* Think about it: The gospel is the only message upon which believers completely agree. Those who proclaim the gospel can be in 100 percent agreement about its core truth.

5. Its *polarizing effect.* Millions reject the gospel precisely because its message is so unambiguous and exclusionary. The parts about *"no other name* but Jesus" and *"all have sinned"* don't seem to sit too well with them.

## A Question of Priority

Ironically, the group with the greatest potential to represent a perpetually unifying message can, if we're not careful, become so inwardly focused and undisciplined with the script that nonbelievers rightly say Christians are anything but unified. How is this possible?

To explain, let's pick a particular opinion or political leaning. How about capitalism versus socialism? Surveys repeatedly indicate American evangelicals have a higher-than-average preference for free-market capitalism. The same group leans in favor of school choice, where tax dollars can travel with students to public, private, or charter schools, however the parents decide. Most of these same Christians register strong opposition to public officials misbehaving sexually.

But those evangelicals who lean conservative on these issues are hardly alone. A great number of Muslims, for example, hold similar views on one or more of those matters. Mormons, Jehovah's Witnesses, and Hindus, to name a few, have many members who feel similarly.

In such cases, we believers are no longer camped in the territory of the exclusive. If we invoke the name of Jesus or

His church in public debates about capitalism, education, or marital fidelity, our conclusions would be common to what some Muslims, Jews, or even atheists might voice.

But along the way, we will have compromised what is truly unique (the gospel) and will have jeopardized the unique reputation of Jesus. In the eyes of nonbelievers, Christianity will have been lowered to the same playing field as other belief systems.

But our message is *not* on par with others; it is exceptional! That is why the early church leaders did not muddy the gospel waters in any fashion before nonbelievers, even when worthwhile causes existed.

In his book *Sinners in the Hands of an Angry Church*, Dean Merrill captures this sentiment with his account of culture under two first-century Roman emperors, Caligula and Nero. Merrill's insightful description includes the nuggets that Caligula was …

> … a brutal tyrant who raised taxes, spent prodigious amounts of money, and murdered the prefect who had helped him get chosen as emperor. In his sexual life, there were no boundaries; Caligula enjoyed the intimacy of both women and men. He was particularly smitten with his three sisters, especially Drusilla, even though she was married to someone else—whom he ordered to be executed.

Merrill then poses questions we must soberly ask.

> What did the early Christians think of Caligula's conduct? They must have been appalled like everyone else.

Did they write letters of protest? Did Peter go back to his newly converted friend Cornelius and say, "Can't you do something about this crazy emperor? I'm only a Jew, but you're part of the Roman military. You have connections. As a Spirit-filled Christian now, you need to use your clout for the defense of righteousness and public decency. What action are you going to take?" The book of Acts is completely silent. Whatever the early believers thought and did about Caligula's disgraceful antics, it wasn't considered significant enough to make it into Luke's history.[34]

And it wasn't just Peter and Cornelius (Acts 10). Remember Jesus and the Roman Centurion (Matthew 8)? How about Paul with the Roman proconsul on Cyprus (Acts 13) or with the jailer in Philippi (Acts 16)? Jesus and the apostles had numerous exchanges with officials in the Roman chain of authority, officials like these who professed faith in Christ. But we never see even a hint of these New Testament preachers invoking the name of Jesus to press for moral or societal changes through government or political channels. Some speculate this silence stemmed from intimidation by community and government leaders, including Caesar himself. Seriously? We know that Peter, Paul and the others boldly proclaimed the gospel (and *just* the gospel) despite frequent episodes of threats, beatings and imprisonment by officials, Jew and Gentile alike.

Is Jesus in favor of government leaders behaving morally, whether in North Korea or North America? Certainly. Is He in favor of babies being protected inside the womb? Of course! Should believers be pro-life and work hard (much more than we seem to be doing) to advance the rights of the unborn and the care for hurting moms and dads? Absolutely! But we can do so, and do it more effectively, when we prioritize the gospel message in its rightful place of design and purpose.

## A Case in Point

Let's take the abortion topic a little further, since it is such a well-known example. God wants to use committed and talented Christ-followers to counteract this horrifying practice and its devastating consequences.

What can be done?

First and foremost, we can address the hurts and struggles with abortion going on *inside* the church, in far greater numbers than you might imagine. One of abortion's darkest secrets is the shockingly high number of procedures that result from Christ-following mothers or fathers driving their daughters to an abortion clinic. They do so reluctantly, often out of embarrassment over a baby being conceived out of wedlock in what was supposed to be a God-honoring home. Consequently, the hidden hurt filling our pews is staggering.

The church can address this! It can offer a greater degree of substantive assistance to pregnant mothers and their families; it can preach and teach about the value of life and forgiveness and the importance of pursuing God's best in our sexual relationships; it can help those in our ranks who have been wounded by past abortions, offering critically valuable guidance and support to fellow believers, one-on-one. All of these actions would have an undeniable impact on the abortion epidemic. Ask any counselor or pro-life professional in the trenches at pregnancy help centers or organizations, and they will tell you that ending abortions today among believing households would result in a seismic drop in the nation's overall abortion rate.

Of course, countless unwanted pregnancies also happen among nonbelievers. Should Christ-followers do something about that? Should we engage in spiritual warfare by regularly praying for abortion to end? Yes! (And while we're at it, would you join me in repenting of our casual attitude about prayer? Instead of mumbling phrases such as "All we can do is pray..." as if it were a last resort, congregations need to pray with zeal and expectation as a first resort! Passionate prioritization of prayer was certainly NTN.)

Now, what about efforts in the public square?

In free societies, Christ-followers can exercise the privilege of electing government officials who will advocate for pro-life policies. Believers living in democratic nations are charged with being productive citizens, living out their faith. Not to be overlooked, this *includes* churches speaking respectfully of public servants. To do otherwise would not be NTN. In fact, it would be counterproductive. We want our own young people to be highly motivated, not turned off, to serve as Christ-honoring judges, teachers, social workers, physicians, police, and elected officials at all levels of government. "Righteousness exalts a nation" (Prov. 14:34).

So while lifting up the name of Jesus as we preach and teach the gospel to nonbelievers, we can also cast our ballots for pro-life candidates, whether they publicly invoke Christianity in their candidacy or not. We can give anti-abortion speeches, donate funds, volunteer, educate voters and use our democratic right to march and protest. Our language, for example, can take one or more of the following effective and legitimate platforms:

"I am partnering with other committed citizens of this country, and we vote."

"I am enthusiastically donating finances and/or my time to assist my local pregnancy help center."

"I have personally experienced the pain of abortion, so I am advocating to prevent others from doing what I did."

What we are *not* communicating in any of these is "We are Jesus people, and so we're against what you're doing."

Some might argue this is akin to being embarrassed of Christ or shirking our Christian responsibilities. To the contrary, it is instead about the resolute determination that Christ's message powerfully transcends and brings illumination to every other issue and heartache known to mankind.

Therefore, we can, and we will, demonstrate today the same discipline the disciplined first-century disciples (devoted followers) of Christ modeled for us. How? By preaching Christ crucified *outside* the church and acting as responsible citizens regardless of the political climate, all while clearly teaching Scripture's take on sin and immorality *inside* the church.

Another way of saying it is this: If we really mean it when we say our hearts are broken about abortion, then may we never neglect what's most effective—winning our world for Jesus. (The same happens to be true, by the way, when "abortion" is swapped out with "sexual sin" or "bigotry" or "drug use.") At the same time, we can have loving, nonjudgmental conversations with nonbelievers (men as well as women) who are personally wrestling with or reeling from an abortion decision. This is what many pregnancy help centers and organizations do so well.

Heartbeat International is a worldwide pro-life organization, currently serving 1,800 affiliated pregnancy help locations, maternity homes, and non-profit adoption agencies on all six inhabited continents. I love the perspective their vice-president, Cindi Boston, shared with me:

> No woman wants an abortion. She only chooses it because she feels so alone and so desperate that it feels as if it is her only choice. Just imagine if the church would really rise up on this critical issue. We are uniquely positioned to provide such incredible love and hope that no Christian would electively choose termination. We can demonstrate the love of Christ and support pro-life efforts so nonbelievers wouldn't feel it necessary either. And, we can talk about after-abortion care from the platform while offering loving, helpful connections so the women sitting in our churches would have the support they need to work through their devastating and often debilitating post-abortion pain and shame.[35]

Does it make any sense to use the name of Christ and His Church to lambast the world about abortion while it remains such a problem inside our churches? (The same is true, of course, for the challenge Christians have with fornication, lying, and gluttony.) Couldn't all believers agree it would be a wise start to lower abortion rates inside the church?

If so, let's keep winning more and more people to Jesus. Let His Spirit change their orientation on living and loving. Then, we can spread the truth about healthy sexual relationships, preventing unwanted pregnancies in the first place, and the value of every human life when our audience is full of people who increasingly see things the way Jesus does!

## Time and Place

Abortion is touchy. So are a lot of other topics associated with choices we make as humans. That's why so many churches provide more than one teaching setting throughout the week. In order for believers to grow in their faith, they arrange for various formats of the "house to house" discipleship we read about in Acts 2:46. This is how conversations can go as deep as they need to. It's how personal questions come to the surface and get addressed.

For decades in many churches, this also took place during a Sunday school hour. It still occurs today, although vast numbers of congregations have shrunk Sunday mornings to a single experience (often repeated with two or more services). To compensate, they offer small groups at other times in a more intimate setting where believers can chew on Scripture and get their questions answered.

Having Sunday school or small groups for believers helps them grow, especially in areas of holiness. There is time and space in these smaller settings to examine biblical directives that explain why marriage is preferred to cohabitating, or why consuming alcohol is such a tricky and potentially devastating habit. In a smaller room full of people who are forgiven, who value the Word of God, these conversations can be led and managed most effectively.

This frees up the main service, or perhaps an evening gathering on another day, for preaching the gospel with nonbelievers in mind. Knowing they themselves were already fed in that smaller setting, believers can come worshiping God and expecting people to get saved as the Holy Spirit does what the Holy Spirit did in the early church.

Have you found it true that people are more likely to let others cut in line at the buffet, and even smile as they do it, when they've already gone through a time or two themselves? Believers who have prayed and worshiped throughout the week are naturally less concerned about the song selection for public services. They care less about their own sound and lighting preferences, because they are increasingly convinced that this service is not driven by what makes them comfortable.

Meanwhile, nonbelievers are more likely to catch a clue that the service they are attending is designed for them to connect with God. This helps them see how attractive Jesus really is. On the other hand, when nonbelievers hear and see Jesus people pushing politics, morality debates, or anything other than the gospel, whether it's from the pulpit, on the church sign out front, or on the church's weekly TV program, we give them an instant excuse to lump our faith in with all the others.

This approach, I have argued in previous chapters, is the Bible way. We don't read in the New Testament about any nonbelievers attending a public service where anything like morality or politics was harped on ... ever. Can you read that again? The disciples kept those settings focused on the gospel. Why would we feel comfortable doing otherwise when there is no biblical basis to do so?

> **We don't read in the New Testament about any nonbelievers attending a public service where anything like morality or politics was harped on ... ever.**

In contrast to Paul and Peter and the others, Western Christians nowadays seem to have such a hard time staying on message. We daily confuse nonbelievers by investing so much energy in the name of Christ to promote a secondary agenda, such as incessantly attacking the film and music industries. Then, we add to the confusion by publicly emphasizing spiritual debates, even arguments against other believers, outside the core of the gospel. With nonbelievers in our audience, we seem to be working overtime to broadcast that Christians are far from being on the same page. What are we thinking?!

Christians critiquing other Christians in front of nonbelievers has already been covered in a previous chapter. My purpose in revisiting the topic here is to point out what a crime that really is. Not only is it a nonbiblical practice (are we ready to call it "sin" yet?), but it also robs us of our greatest asset in spreading a uniquely unifying gospel. Speaking ill of other believers or contradicting their spiritual views while nonbelievers have a front-row seat hardly allows Christ's disciples to be known by their love for one another.

## Tone Matters

In addition to the New Testament mandate for believers to stay focused on the exclusively good news of Jesus Christ, there is also a mandate about our demeanor in the process. The more off-point our dialog becomes, the greater our chances for violating a clear pattern of instruction about the aroma we leave as believers.

Repeated New Testament passages leave no room for us to speak with a sour tone in front of nonbelievers. To quote just a few:

- Let your light so shine before men that they may see your good works and glorify your Father who is in heaven. (Matthew 5:16)
- Walk in wisdom toward those who are outside, wisely using the opportunity. Let your speech always be with grace, seasoned with salt, that you may know how you should answer everyone. (Colossians 4:5-6)
- If it is possible, as much as it depends on you, live peaceably with all men. (Romans 12:18)
- Remind them to be subject to rulers and authorities, to obey them, to be ready for every good work, to speak evil of no one, not to be contentious, but gentle, showing all humility toward everyone. (Titus 3:1-2)

This is how we score one victory after another. We maximize Jesus and make Him supremely attractive. We get people onto the citizen rolls of heaven. We swell the ranks of the church, which makes the church stronger and more able to shine light into the world, corporately and individually. We take the focus off of us and our demands, putting all the attention on the incredible invitation our loving heavenly Father extends.

Quite likely, as a byproduct, we then see the positive societal results that have eluded the church for decades and centuries: born-again converts who no longer want anything to do with the abuse of drugs or alcohol ... new believers who start to realize they cannot continue cohabitating without being married in the eyes of God ... a growing army of saints who are less greedy and more interested in helping their neighbor ... annual health reports that start showing fewer sexually transmitted diseases and unwanted pregnancies ... a growing number of political candidates and government leaders with Christ inside them, guiding their votes and their platforms. We forsake our snide remarks about candidates with whom we disagree. We abandon our attempts to pressure nonbelievers to adopt our moral codes. We say, "Never again!" to the temptation to throw shade on a fellow believer, especially when non-Christians can see us doing it.

## Wandering Off Script

In addition to the many positive New Testament examples I have cited throughout this book, let me go on to examine what happened after the New Testament was written.

We're not the only generation of believers who went off script, forsaking the exclusive nature of the gospel. Historians, both pagan and Christian, indicate that the church and its influence continued to rise for several centuries after Pentecost—so much so that Emperor Constantine in the early fourth century A.D. used his power to spread, and even mandate, Christian allegiance. Paul and Peter, of course, were long dead by then.

This rising power and influence in government and culture, previously unknown to Christ's disciples, was not always easy to navigate. It appears Christians had gone off script as early as the end of the second century, according to Rodney Stark. Though previously silent on social issues ...

> Christians were not only proclaiming their rejection of abortion and infanticide, but had begun direct attacks on pagans, and especially pagan religions, for sustaining such "crimes." In his *Octavius*, Minucius Felix charged: And I see that you at one time expose your begotten

children to wild beasts and to birds; at another, that you crush when strangled with a miserable kind of death. There are some women [among you] who, by drinking medical preparations, extinguish the source of the future man in their very bowels, and thus commit a parricide before they bring forth. And these things assuredly come down from your gods. For Saturn did not expose his children, but devoured them. With reason were infants sacrificed to him in some parts of Africa.[36]

Significant segments of Christianity took some regrettable turns after the first several centuries. Believers who gained influence in government and society needed to resist the tendency to overreach. Mandating religious and moral allegiance by nonbelievers, to the point of persecution, was hardly NTN.

Infanticide, such as mentioned above, is indeed a horrendous atrocity. Without question, we ignore the heart of the gospel if we fail to call all sinners to repentance, and this clearly includes those who take the life of innocent babies. But baby killers who stop killing babies, even when the law permits them to do otherwise, can still miss out on heaven if they are without Christ. Anyone who has not yet admitted they are a sinner in need of a Savior, whose name is Jesus Christ, needs to repent as soon as possible. Repenting of a sinful heart and turning to God is the main conversation. And it's a different conversation than figuring out why ending a life in the womb is so tragic or why casual sex is such a harmful habit.

Indeed, the New Testament contains dozens of references to repenting, including repeated instances where nonbelievers are urged to do so.

- Jesus: Repent! For the Kingdom of heaven is at hand. (Matthew 4:17)
- Peter: Repent and be baptized, every one of you, in the name of Jesus Christ for the forgiveness of sins, and you shall receive the gift of the Holy Spirit. (Acts 2:38)
- Paul: But now God commands all men everywhere to repent. (Acts 17:30)

Over and over again, the NTN plea to repent is in general gospel terms, with no reference to moral shortcomings, like fornication or profanity. With the Ephesian believers as his firsthand witnesses, Paul summarized his ministry, to both Jews and Gentiles, by saying he taught repentance toward God and faith in our Lord Jesus Christ (Acts 20:21). Now does it surprise you to learn that not one time were nonbelievers in Ephesus, or anywhere, told by Paul to repent from a specific immoral behavior? No mention of their vulgarities or dressing immodestly. Not even the immoral practice of tagging friends and family on Facebook with the annoying challenge of the month. (I jest, of course. Kind of.)

In all of the New Testament, there *are* two direct examples of believers urging repentance from sexual sin or indecency. The first is in 2 Corinthians 12:21 and the second is in Revelation 2:18-25. Consistent with NTN practice, however, these are both addressed toward Christians who are committing these acts, *not* unbelievers. There is no exception to this. I propose it is an indisputable pattern of instruction and experience.

In fact, this is the flow of the entire Bible. From the Old Testament, through the Gospels, to the end of Revelation. Before the law was given, after it was given, and after Christ's sacrifice, the message has been consistent. Old Testament Jew or New Testament Christian: If you already have a relationship with God and you are violating His commands, repent! If you don't yet serve God, repent for worshiping yourself or any other false god. Receive His love, and discover your highest purpose, on earth and in heaven.

Challenging nonbelievers over immoral behavior does not represent the exclusive and exceptional gospel. Such practice has no foundation in Jesus and His apostles. These powerful lyrics from the Christian band Casting Crowns poignantly sum up our dilemma, and our prayer:

Jesus, Friend of sinners
We have strayed so far away
We cut down people in your name
But the sword was never ours to swing
Jesus, Friend of sinners
The truth's become so hard to see
The world is on their way to You
But they're tripping over me
Always looking around but never looking up
I'm so double-minded
A plank-eyed saint with dirty hands and a heart divided

Oh Jesus, Friend of sinners
Open our eyes to the world at the end of our pointing fingers
Let our hearts be led by mercy
Help us reach with open hearts and open doors
Oh Jesus, Friend of sinners
Break our hearts for what breaks yours[37]

How do we cut down sinners in His name? Perhaps one of the strongest cases to be made is the devastating lack of context a setting like immorality debates always fosters. When we keep the focus on Jesus, we never run the risk of Him embarrassing our cause. In His love, power, and perfection, He *is* our cause! But when we take a detour into arguments about lifestyle choices and sins, we unwisely set up our own morality and that of our fellow believers as the imperfect standard instead.

You've seen it too often, unfortunately ... and so has the world. It happens countless times in smaller circles like families and churches. But the failures on the big stage garner the most attention. Famous characters such as TV preachers and celebrities use the name of Jesus and Christianity as their platform for openly and harshly criticizing sinners and their questionable mores. Then, not surprisingly, their occasional falls from grace are typically tragic and public.

People without Jesus or God's Word inside them have little context for understanding why forgiven people who are on their way to heaven could have moments when their actions fall considerably short of their message. All they know is what they see ... and they're right. "He was the captain of the Morals Police, then he just did exactly what he's been telling everyone else not to do. There's one more in a very long line of Christian hypocrites!"

Instead of tripping nonbelievers on their way to Jesus, believers can share a clarifying gospel message that has no equal. When the hearts of hurting sinners in need of healing are turned to Jesus first, their struggles with various vices can be conquered by Calvary's cure. Victory over old habits will be gained quickly by some, more slowly by others.

Further, each new believer discovers that triumph over some challenges arrives more quickly than triumph over other struggles. The crazy and unique path we each once took on our journey into sin should prepare us not to be surprised that our journey out will also be a process, and it will be unique to us.

But what a difference new life via the gospel can be, compared to the painful on-again off-again cycles that entrap sinners without God's Spirit living inside. With this in focus, our priority emphasis must remain on first attracting sinners to the foot of the cross.

After all, the gospel is the one message the world can get from us that they can't get anywhere else. There's already an abundant supply of debates. Pressure. Moralizing. Campaigning. Hypocrisy. Arguments. Guilt.

The gospel, on the other hand, is unique in its message, its power, its beauty, and its Author. May God's Word inspire us and may His Spirit empower us to rediscover the gospel's unparalleled potential. As a result, may believers increasingly devote themselves to a pattern of messaging that reflects a deeper appreciation for the unifying gospel we have been given, and which the world needs now more than ever.

# GET THE MESSAGE?

The gospel is simultaneously the world's most inclusive and exclusive story. All are welcome at the Father's table, but none may enter without a repentant heart devoted to Jesus as Lord.

Believers can inadvertently diminish the exceptional nature of the gospel by using the name of Jesus to passionately promote social causes and moral values already associated with many atheists as well as followers of Islam and other religions.

Whether a nation is led by despots or presidents, Christian citizens all have varying degrees of opportunity and responsibility to be productive contributors toward a better society without always invoking Christianity in their push for change.

The most effective means for believers to confront immorality is to do so inside the church. Churches who keep winning sinners to Jesus will have a nonstop supply of filth to challenge and clean up, right there in their very own pews.

We don't read in the New Testament about any nonbelievers attending a public service where anything like morality or politics was harped on ... ever.

In dozens of New Testament references to repentance, only two call for repentance from sexual sin or indecency, and both are directed at believers.

# 10

# WHAT EVERY BELIEVER CAN DO

Lack of knowledge? Misguided passion? I've been asking myself what drives me in certain moments to want to lash out at others.

Until recently, I had never studied the specific patterns of instructions and experience highlighted in this book. So ignorance certainly played a role. And I certainly have a passion to see others, whether believers or unbelievers, enjoy the benefits of walking properly in God's eyes. Steering people away from unhealthy and destructive habits is rooted in many truly noble aspirations.

But what if, in the end, there is more at play here than just good intentions gone awry, as I initially proposed? What if there were more than a few moments when what really inspired me was a more serious character flaw? Is it possible I've repeatedly used manipulation for the sake of my own comfort? Has my selfishness somehow masqueraded as righteousness?

I am growing more convinced that this is part of the driving force behind many Christians like me operating outside the boundaries of NTN instruction and experience. In many cases, we've become incredibly deft at hiding our motivations from our own hearts.

Why am I drawn like a moth to the flame, like a yuppie to Starbucks, to speak out publicly against Christians who take a different approach than I do in living out their faith? Why does it just feel so right to tell sinners how messed up they are on the transgender issue?

Why? Because, in part, my comfort level is threatened. If I'm completely honest, I would admit the truth. I do feel much more at ease when I see fellow believers adopting the same approach I do in viewing God and the world. It reduces my stress significantly when most Americans signal by their own actions and reactions that my general outlook about what's right and what's wrong with this country jibes with theirs.

"No, no!" you object. "You're jumping to conclusions. Christians speak out because they so desperately want to see people avoid the pain that comes with unrighteous behavior." Perhaps, for some believers, at first. But with decades, even centuries, of hard evidence proving the abject failure of trying to pressure nonbelievers into adopting Christian morals, without biblical support for doing so, does that rationale really hold up?

Maybe if we scream louder this time. Maybe if we hold public rallies. Maybe if we craft a better boycott. Maybe if we get our candidate elected. Maybe if I get red in the face and quote a Bible passage (out of context) to support my personal preference.

You know the oft-quoted definition of insanity, right? *Doing the same thing over and over while expecting different results.*

We know full well that Christians in other places are having the effect we long for by taking a radically different approach. So why do we keep pounding away at efforts that keep producing the opposite result we are hoping for?

Why do we labor for courts to outlaw same-sex marriage but not heterosexual adultery? Are sexually deviant heterosexuals in any less danger of hell fire than practicing homosexuals?

Why do we lose sleep worrying if people will choose our candidate but not our Savior?

## Dream On ...

I would be much more comfortable, of course, if the people behind the Oval Office desk, in the halls of Congress, and on the Supreme Court bench interpreted the Bible the way I do. I would love it if the spiritually twisted and morally bankrupt politicians would all resign. I wish protesters who burn the flag would be less demonstrative. Yeah, and while we're at it, I wish Michigan Wolverines fans would just see the light and root for the Ohio State Buckeyes. That would increase my comfort. But do I weep in intercession that they would fall in love with my Jesus?

In the wildest fantasy of many evangelicals (not all, of course), misbehaving people need to just cut it out. Illegal immigrants should all voluntarily go back home and wait in line. Members of irritating social justice groups need to quit causing such a distraction. Gays should become straight, or at least stay in their closets. Bureaucrats should never push for massive government healthcare. TV meteorologists should admit

> **Why do we lose sleep worrying if people will choose our candidate but not our Savior?**

global warming is a hoax. Boards of education need to abandon safe-sex curriculum and evolution propaganda, replacing them with classes on Second Amendment freedoms.

Though the likelihood seems low that any of these wishes will come true, what if they actually did? In fact, what if they all did? Wouldn't that be great!

It *would* be great ... for me. Of course, I'm already on my way to heaven; nothing has changed in that regard. But at least my here-and-now world would be a little less stressful. Whew!

But not so great for them. The cart got before the horse somewhere. True, they might start avoiding some of the lifestyles and attitudes that I find disturbing. They might sidestep lung cancer if they quit smoking. They could be spared from the devastating effects of sexually transmitted diseases.

But without Jesus, countless souls would still be very much on a custom-crafted fast track to a Christless eternity. And *that* is what breaks God's heart.

The early disciples never allowed passion for social comfort to approach their zeal for seeing people saved. It wasn't even close. Consider, again, a clarifying insight from Dr. Rodney Stark in which he pulls the curtain back on one of the places the apostles visited often, where the church was firmly established, and where Western believers like us might feel a little uncomfortable.

Any accurate portrait of Antioch in New Testament times must depict a city filled with misery, danger, fear, despair, and hatred. A city where the average family lived a squalid life in filthy and cramped quarters, where at least half of the children died at birth or during infancy, and where most of the children who lived lost at least one parent before reaching maturity. A city filled with hatred and fear rooted in intense ethnic antagonisms and exacerbated by a constant stream of strangers. A city so lacking in stable networks of attachments that petty incidents could prompt mob violence. A city where crime flourished and the streets were dangerous at night. And, perhaps above all, a city repeatedly smashed by cataclysmic catastrophes: where a resident could expect literally to be homeless from time to time, providing that he or she was among the survivors.[38]

Lovely. And, yet, with all their visits to Antioch, we don't see the disciples deviating one iota from preaching the gospel. Why? Because the best remedy for what ails any society, then and now, will always be to prioritize salvation through faith in Jesus Christ.

## Ranks in Disarray

In the previous chapter, we discussed the perils of allowing the Christian church's social messaging to be seen as parallel with other non-Christian religions. Unfortunately, that was just the warm-up act. It's actually worse than that.

In what is perhaps the ultimate self-inflicted wound, too many Christians represent the gospel in a fashion that directly contradicts its unifying essence. We can't seem to quit messaging nonbelievers that the church is just as messed up and confused as everyone else.

What do I mean?

Predominantly white churches in suburban and especially rural settings, for example, have not been bashful about promoting the candidacies of Republicans, while predominantly black churches frequently push for Democrats. Both groups use their pulpits to make their cases, happy to influence as many voters as possible, regardless of their faith condition. This is true not just in and around their congregation but at political rallies and on cable news whenever possible, without being ashamed to inject Scripture in the process. Blatantly partisan prayers passionately invoking God's favor on the elections of Hillary Clinton and Donald Trump were offered in prime time by Christians at both the 2016 Republican and Democratic conventions. Were Christians convinced that God apparently wanted *both* Clinton and Trump elected?

With nonbelievers watching, older believers take to social media with postings of articles on why rejection of all alcohol is the only position acceptable in God's eyes. Then those rebellious Christian millennials push back. They even have the audacity to quote a few Scriptures themselves. Who raised them, anyway?

People who all agree that Jesus is Savior disagree about the approach we take to many other issues! Gun rights versus gun control. Racial tensions. Clemency versus the death penalty. Amnesty. Gays in the church. Muslim refugees. Welfare and universal healthcare. The list of our disputes, of course, is endless. And we keep going public, Jesus-follower versus Jesus-follower, throwing in a Scripture verse or two along the way just for good measure. Nonbelievers observe all this and accurately conclude that Jesus people fight dirty with each other just like everyone else. Why in the world would they want what we have, when they already have more than enough of it on their own?

As surprising and disappointing as it always is to discover, there are well-intentioned believers who are forgiven by Jesus and on their way to heaven who—gasp!—don't have the same worldview that I do on every issue. I will actually be worshiping God forever with these people. So, I can start acting like I understand that, or I can keep using the name of Jesus to push my preferred moral or political agenda. Of course, that will only incite other Jesus-followers to push an agenda contrary to mine. And the world will keep getting confused, and turned off!

But since the gospel message actually unites us, what if we started behaving now like we would in the best of times? If our church was growing by virtue of a regular influx of new converts, we would have our hands full. We'd be so busy cleaning up new believers we wouldn't have time to bother Starbucks about the design on their Christmas cups. We could invest our time answering questions from people who are actually eager to hear God's plan for their sex lives. Doesn't that sound a little more on-mission than rallying Christians to teach Target stores a lesson about God's theology on retail bathrooms? Heaven keeps pointing to the Great Commission and saying, "Um, you had one job."

If that's not motivation enough, let's consider another scenario. What if it were the worst of times? What if, as many Christian leaders have been predicting for decades, our civil liberties were stripped away? If that day is coming—it may well be—wouldn't it behoove us to act now to be prepared? The least we can do with all this forewarning is to not be caught off guard when we can no longer worship in public or share the gospel openly.

We certainly couldn't sound off about other Christians then! To do so, to publicly ridicule a precious teammate, might put their very life in jeopardy by identifying them as a follower of Christ. In numerous hostile nations it already has, for decades. And even sharing Scripture with nonbelievers would be incredibly risky. Maybe that's why, throughout history and even in many territories today, persecuted believers and missionaries waste little time with the private lives of nonbelievers. When every word matters, and carries the risk of imprisonment or worse, Christ-followers tend to focus on the eternal: choose Jesus.

This is the paradox of the often unstated rebuttals to the topics highlighted in this book. In general, it seems those bent on calling out fellow Christians and nonbelievers do so with gusto. For many, it is obvious in their claims that they believe they are the strong, obedient, and righteous ones, and the seemingly silent types are too timid to do what God has *really* told us all to do.

But wouldn't the account of Scripture bear out the opposite to be true? When disciples stayed on message, persecution did not escape them. In many cases, it came looking for them! Hear again this familiar testimony from Paul, but this time, appreciate it as the account of someone who continually preached Christ crucified while never once rebuking nonbelievers for sporting tattoos or pole dancing.

> I am ... in labors more abundant, in stripes above measure, in prisons more frequently, in deaths often. Five times I received from the Jews forty lashes minus one. Three times I was beaten with rods; once I was stoned; three times I suffered shipwreck; a night and a day I have been in the deep; in journeys often, in perils of waters, in perils of robbers, in perils by my own countrymen, in perils by the

Gentiles, in perils in the city, in perils in the wilderness, in perils in the sea, in perils among false brothers; in weariness and painfulness, in sleeplessness often, in hunger and thirst, in fastings often, and in cold and nakedness. (2 Corinthians 11:23-27)

When we stand up for Jesus without wavering, we may well garner more attention from the enemies of the cross than when we try to convert sinners to the glories of Republican heterosexuality. Wait, forgive me—*gun-toting* Republican heterosexuality. Got it that time. Protesting for rainbow-waving Democratic environmentalism doesn't seem to rattle hell either. I wonder why that is. Could it be that everything we know except the souls of men and women will one day be destroyed?

When I see a saint who stays on script, I admire their incredible courage. Man or woman, they are declaring their allegiance to winning people for Christ. And slapping one huge target on their backs in the process.

Great times. Horrible times. Open societies. Rigid dictatorships. A.D. 50 or A.D. 2050. God's plan is the same: to see all the players on the other team defect to His. He's far more interested in depleting their bench than defeating their bench.

How do we do our part to stay on script?

- Love people like crazy, especially our teammates.
- Handle sin and conflict in stages, inside the church.
- Tell the world why the cross is such good news.
- Clean the fish after we catch them, not before.

How could believers go wrong with this approach? The biblical patterns of instruction and experience are overwhelmingly in support. If nothing else, I hope readers are equipped for the next discussion they have on this topic. It's time to start asking questions when we see non-NTN behaviors on display.

Scripture is clear: Believers pray. They worship. They absorb God's Word. They live holy lives. They work really hard at meeting people at their level. And they consistently keep a watch on their audience, choosing their words accordingly.

## Ten Moratoriums

Remember earlier when I poked fun at my naïveté? Common sense tells me a more realistic aspiration than an all-out "Moratorium" might be to plea for at least a "Less-atorium." Any movement in the NTN direction is a good thing! These paradigm shifts often take baby steps. Nonetheless, in addition to proactively spreading the gospel through every means possible, here are Ten Moratoriums for consideration:

1. Can Christian media (television, radio, magazines, and publishing houses, including their online presence) cease and desist from providing public platforms for believers to so easily and inappropriately trash each other in view of nonbelievers?

2. Can the same folks stop facilitating Christians who insist on lecturing nonbelievers about their immorality and politics instead of wooing them to our incredible Savior? I notice positive signs that younger believers are picking this up and running with it. Innovations will come

sooner if we invite them to the table of influence and decision-making.

3. Can Christian pastors and leaders quit ignoring our responsibility to hold Christian media outlets more accountable in this regard? All it would take is a few churches to start e-mailing their executives every time they foster an outburst in conflict with Matthew 18.

4. Can Christian speakers, preachers, pastors, evangelists, and authors quit sounding off on "the flavor of the month" (this sexual sin or that cultural trend) and focus on the gospel instead, when we know there's a good chance the message will be seen by nonbelievers? This heightens the need for congregations to embrace and celebrate the NTN distinction between settings for believers only versus settings where nonbelievers are expected.

   There are no guarantees, of course, that nonbelievers won't hear; that's an impractical expectation. Even the New Testament refers to settings where nonbelievers snuck into gatherings for believers. But the point is to shift and clarify our emphasis.

5. Can Christian leaders who've ignored the rampant sin problems in the church start preaching for holiness with renewed zeal and hunger? For the next decade or two, could we test these principles and see what happens? What if we talked and warned more than ever about adultery and gluttony and gossip and sexual deviation of all kinds, but did it in the confines of smaller, more intimate audiences whose members already love Jesus? People who call Jesus their Lord are committing acts of

adultery and lesbianism every week. Let's help them see what Scripture says! They're falsifying their timesheets, boasting to high heaven, and coveting their co-worker's wife. We've already got a full-time job admonishing and helping more people with their sins than we can shake a stick at. We've just been aiming outside the church instead of inside, where our focus belongs, and where it would be the most productive.

6. Can the rest of us, "in the pews," do our part on social media? Can we stop egging others on? Can we ignore those errant and derogatory posts on Twitter and Facebook, especially when believers don't sound very much like the salt and light Christ said we would be? Instead of getting something off our chest for the sake of venting (or more accurately, *vomiting*), how about a new paradigm? Instead of sharing with the whole world why certain believers upset or disappoint us, why not post some agenda-free praise for a worthy high-profile believer. When appropriate, champion their love for Jesus and one another, which is agenda #1 and #2, after all. Next time there's a natural calamity, give kudos publicly to the Christian charities who are saving lives and bringing comfort in the name of Jesus.

7. Can we refuse to skip the first vital steps of Matthew 18 when a brother or sister sins against us? Before we tell one person, even our pastor, what another believer has done wrong, can we take one second to rewind the tape? Is this actually about a sin or is it more about a preference or a style? Did we meet with the person yet? If that didn't work, did we try again? If that didn't

work, did we try it again with a witness or two? Can we quickly and directly confront the next person who posts an open letter critiquing another believer? Even (and I'd say, *especially*) if they include the disclaimer, "I tried reaching out to them but got no reply." Wow—as if that caveat comes even close to cutting the mustard in light of Scripture. We're better than that. The eternities of the nonbelievers watching are way more important than that!

8. Can we immediately withdraw our financial support from Western preachers or ministries who refuse to operate under the authority of a board that can hold them accountable? It's the twenty-first century, and operating independent of legitimate accountability is unacceptable. When no oversight board is present or advertised, especially for high profile believers, those desiring to voice concerns about the minister's teaching or behavior are less likely to select a healthy channel of communication, opting for a social media tirade instead. Before you make that donation online, do you have assurance that the board is not controlled by the preacher's family? Are the board members simply "yes men" who are appointed (and unappointed) by the charismatic personality whose face you see on screen?

Thankfully, many well-known preachers and evangelists have gone to great lengths to remain above reproach when it comes to the serious matter of kingdom accountability and finances. Their reputations, and the reputation of the church at large, are seriously damaged by unscrupulous charlatans. The least we can do is stop facilitating those characters who willfully ignore their responsibility to place themselves under some type of legitimate spiritual authority.

9. When discussing issues better reserved for believers, can Christian bloggers and website hosts quit using platforms accessible by whosoever will? Closed and secret pages utilized by online groups have existed for years. This is hardly new technology.

   I am not advocating the withholding of vital information and scriptural insights from brothers and sisters in Christ who need it. Believers everywhere benefit from online resources and the Internet is an irreplaceable lifeline for saints limited by travel, health or restrictions on religion. But it is entirely possible to minimize the non-gospel rhetoric we keep indiscriminately throwing in front of nonbelievers. If you haven't already done so, ask the administrator of your online group if any effort has been made to verify that all members are believers. It may mean that your group needs to be disbanded and relaunched with a new verification process. Do it!

10. Can all of us (this author most definitely included) stop living the kind of hypocritical lives that Jesus and others in the New Testament so often warned against? May a spirit of holy sobriety take over all our lives. Lord, forgive my trespasses today and lead me not into temptation. Help me remember to ask for forgiveness regularly, because I will surely need to. If I have any hope of cleaning other fish, help me not neglect the beam in my own eye!

## Focusing Our Spotlight

While I am clearly writing this book because of abundant evidence that we are too often going off script, I also see encouraging signs. After one or two exhausting and defeating experiences with Facebook arguments, many believers realize there must be a better way. Let's not beat ourselves up too badly. It takes a while to learn how to use new tools.

Not long ago, a dear friend of our family who is a great-grandmother in her seventies apologized to her Facebook friends for a misunderstanding. Apparently, Nellie had thought she was encouraging those who had hospital stays or who had lost loved ones by posting "I'm praying for you," then always adding a cheery "LOL." But then she had a revelation courtesy of her grandson. "I'm so sorry everyone," she now wrote. "Please forgive me! My grandson just told me that 'LOL' means 'laughing out loud,' not 'lots of love.'"

Whoa, Nellie! We've been sounding off, it seems, as quickly as an upsetting thought comes to our mind. Filled with passion, like Nellie, we thought we were saying something righteous or helpful. But maybe the only one laughing out loud has been the Devil, who deceived us. We have more tools at our fingertips to act out on our fears and frustrations than ever. But simply because *we can* doesn't mean *we should* or *we must*.

The healthy and abundant scriptural patterns for letting our audience steer our messaging can radically galvanize the unity of Christ's body as never before, helping us turn our two billion randomly directed flashlights (how impractical and irritating is that!) into one brilliant spotlight that stays on mission. More than anything, I want to point the world to our victorious Savior, who is coming oh so soon. And I know you do, too.

# GET THE MESSAGE?

Believers have to question whether our selfishness might be masquerading as righteousness in our efforts to see nonbelievers start adopting our morality or political persuasions before Jesus starts residing in their hearts and minds.

Even if nonbelievers somehow chose to make daily life more comfortable for believers, they would still be on their way to a Christless eternity unless they embrace the gospel.

Believers who use Jesus to push for social, political, or moral advances always incite believers with contrary views to broadcast why the Bible actually supports their cause instead, cementing in the minds of nonbelievers that Christians are just as mixed up as everyone else.

There are at least ten broad approaches people of faith should reconsider in our messaging to nonbelievers.

How do we do our part to stay on script with the teachings and practices of Jesus and the apostles?

- Love people like crazy, especially our teammates.
- Handle sin and conflict in stages, inside the church.
- Tell the world why the cross is such good news.
- Clean the fish after we catch them, not before.

# ENDNOTES

1 http://www.wsj.com/articles/
SB10001424052748703386704576186520353326558

2 https://www.washingtonpost.com/news/acts-of-faith/wp/
2015/12/05/liberty-university-president-if-more-good-people-had-
concealed-guns-we-could-end-those-muslims/

3 http://www.wheatonrecord.com/news/an-open-letter-to-leaders-
in-the-evangelical-community/

4 http://www.chicagotribune.com/news/ct-wheaton-college-falwell-
letter-met-20151210-story.html

5 http://www.cnn.com/2016/05/09/living/methodist-clergy-lgbt/

6 http://www.christianpost.com/news/creflo-dollar-marvin-sapp-to-
join-td-jakes-and-joel-osteen-at-megafest-2013-97473/

7 http://abcnews.go.com/WNT/video/pastor-creflo-dollar-world-
changers-church-fire-29683548

8 http://www.cnn.com/2015/04/23/us/creflo-dollar-jet-response/

9 http://www.ajc.com/news/news/creflo-dollars-lofty-plan-
seeks-65m-jet-for-global/nkWJN/

10 http://www.cbsnews.com/news/televangelist-creflo-dollar-under-
scrutiny-asking-for-65-million-private-jet/

11 http://www.nytimes.com/2016/08/04/world/europe/pope-francis-
remarks-disappoint-gay-and-transgender-groups.html?_r=0

12 http://www.usatoday.com/story/life/tv/2014/02/16/snake-
salvation-pastor-dead/5532531/

13 https://www.washingtonpost.com/lifestyle/style/serpent-
handling-pastor-profiled-earlier-in-washington-post-dies-from-
rattlesnake-bite/2012/05/29/gJQAJef5zU_story.html

[14] Ben Witherington III, *Reading and Understanding the Bible* (New York: Oxford, 2015), 208.

[15] http://www.christianpost.com/news/victoria-osteen-ripped-for-telling-church-just-do-good-for-your-own-self-worship-is-not-for-god-youre-doing-it-for-yourself-125636/

[16] http://www.theblaze.com/stories/2014/09/05/exclusive-victoria-osteen-responds-to-evangelical-furor-over-viral-youre-not-doing-it-for-god-clip/

[17] http://www.huffingtonpost.com/2014/09/04/victoria-osteen-reactions_n_5759860.html333

[18] http://www.chron.com/life/houston-belief/article/Christians-berate-Victoria-Osteen-s-cheap-5736127.php

[19] http://www.wsj.com/articles/SB122965524929320865

[20] http://www.ocregister.com/news/warren-103331-obama-drake.html

[21] http://www.billoreilly.com/b/More-on-the-County-Clerk-in-Kentucky---and-Christianity/565920460838362747.html

[22] Cited at http://www.liberalamerica.org/2015/09/12/open-letter-from-baptist-pastor-destroys-hypocrite-kim-davis-and-her-supporters/

[23] http://www.nytimes.com/2014/10/18/us/megachurch-pastor-signals-shift-in-tone-on-gay-marriage.html?_r=0

[24] https://www.firstthings.com/blogs/firstthoughts/2014/10/a-church-in-exile

[25] http://wchstv.com/news/local/high-school-students-hold-revivial-at-mingo-central-high-school

[26] Rodney Stark, *The Rise of Christianity* (San Francisco: Harper, 1997), 86.

[27] Apology 39 (1989 ed.), cited by Stark, *The Rise of Christianity,* 87.

28 https://www.washingtonpost.com/news/acts-of-faith/wp/2015/05/20/think-christianity-is-dying-no-christianity-is-shifting-dramatically/

29 http://www.pewforum.org/2015/04/02/religious-projections-2010-2050/

30 https://www.washingtonpost.com/news/worldviews/wp/2013/10/17/this-map-shows-where-the-worlds-30-million-slaves-live-there-are-60000-in-the-u-s/

31 Cited by Everett Ferguson, *Backgrounds of Early Christianity*—3rd ed. (Grand Rapids, Mich.: Eerdmans, 1994), 81.

32 © 2016 Billy Graham Evangelistic Association. Used with permission. All rights reserved.

33 https://www.youtube.com/watch?v=ETYEYC-TeEc

34 Dean Merrill, *Sinners in the Hands of an Angry Church* (Grand Rapids, Mich.: Zondervan, 1997), 33-34.

35 One-to-one phone call with the author

36 Stark, *The Rise of Christianity,* 125.

37 http://www.metrolyrics.com/jesus-friend-of-sinners-lyrics-casting-crowns.html

38 Stark, *The Rise of Christianity,* 160.